SILENT SAVIOR

(Daring to Believe He's Still There)

A.J. GREGORY

Revell

a division of Baker Publishing Group
Grand Rapids, Michigan

© 2009 by A. J. Gregory

Published by Revell
a division of Baker Publishing Group
P.O. Box 6287, Grand Rapids, MI 49516-6287
www.revellbooks.com

Printed in the United States of America

Library of Congress Cataloging-in-Publication Data
Gregory, A. J., 1976–
   Silent Savior : (daring to believe He's still there) / A. J. Gregory.
      p. cm.
   Includes bibliographical references (p.   ).
   ISBN 978-0-8007-3285-1 (pbk.)
    1. Spiritual life—Christianity. 2. Hidden God. I. Title.
   BV4509.5.G683 2009
   248.4—dc22   2009016873

Published in association with the literary agency of Fedd & Company, Inc., 9759 Concord Pass, Brentwood, Tennessee 37027.

To my dad:
I'll never stop loving you

Contents

Acknowledgments

Thanks . . .

Esther, you believed in *Silent Savior* when it was just a few pages of an idea about ten years ago. Your prompting and encouragement paved the way to make the dream real. I'll never forget that.

Everyone at Revell who had a hand in making *Silent Savior* what it is. Jennifer Leep, Kristin Kornoelje, all the editors, marketing, sales, and publicity people—thank you to everybody who pitched in. You guys are amazing! There is some supercreative and hardworking talent at Revell, and I am thankful that I am on board with these wonderful people.

Introduction

Perhaps the greatest belief is believing when you
don't see any miracles, visions, or signs of tangible
hope, but you are teeter-tottering on the ledge of
utter unbelief. Belief in spite of the nothingness just
might be where the greatest faith is found. "Lord, I
believe, help Thou my unbelief."

God has never commanded me to remove my flip-flops while
I stared at a burning bush in my backyard. My stuttering
prayers are rarely rewarded with warm and fuzzy feelings.
I have not had my spiritual walk consistently christened
with clear direction through prophetic words, unmistakable
guidance through dreams, or miracles by traveling prophets.
These are things some think should be continually present to
solidify faith in the Unknown. If that is true, I should have
jumped off this spiritual roller coaster years ago. But I still
believe in God, with the sweet mixture of faith and doubt
and with such mysterious abandon that I cannot imagine my
life without this belief.

What happens when God doesn't respond to prayers and desperate questions? What happens when God seems to be at work in the lives of our peers but not in our own? What happens when we knock fervently on heaven's door and all we have to show for it are bruised knuckles, a heart that seems to have been abandoned, and the absence of even a whisper? What happens when we are crucified by the church for struggling to find a balance between faith and doubt, questions and answers? This is the crux of the journey in *Silent Savior*—the whats, the whys, the hows, and the ultimate hope that exists for those who find themselves surrounded by God's silence.

Although in the deepest crevasse of our hearts we may know God is present, we can still hear the trickle of doubts dripping out of our faith's leaky faucet. We all have been through different types of struggles, situations, and ordinary day-to-day living and have experienced the heart-sinking and gut-wrenching feelings of despondency when God seems to be hidden. Though silent seasons are a commonality in the life of any honest Christian, they don't have to be a breeding ground for our faith—or lack thereof.

"How long, O LORD, must I call for help, but you do not listen?" (Hab. 1:2 NIV). This type of desperate questioning is not an uncommon occurrence in the lives of God's children. Flip through the Bible and you'll find a plethora of people mirroring the same frustration birthed from encountering the silent Savior's spiritual iron curtain. Can you imagine the depth of King David's cries when his enemies were on his heels seeking vengeance and God seemed to be taking a nap? Or how about John the Baptist in chains behind iron bars, disheartened at the thought that Jesus had still never proved he was the Messiah? Jesus never even paid John a friendly visit before he was beheaded, nor did he offer him a jolly message to assuage his doubts. "Blessed is the man who is not offended by me," Jesus says—through messengers, no less (see Matt. 11:6). Perhaps, blessed is he who does not keep a grudge and lose faith because he doesn't get the response he is looking for, if he is lucky enough to get a response at all.

And perhaps the most poignant example of them all was the Savior himself, a bloody wreck nailed on a cross in front of a world that thought he was a liar, crazy, or perhaps even the Truth. "My God, my God, why have you forsaken me?" (Matt. 27:46 NIV). Today the Savior's words echo through the struggling man who wonders if his faith is a sick joke, through the parents who have just buried their five-year-old daughter, through the lives of Christians who struggle because they can't get it right, and through folks who suffer from addictions that just won't go away.

From a personal perspective, I have looked for tips and tricks to attract God's attention. Prayer was the obvious choice, of course, but the standard duo of talking and listening didn't seem to work. So began my search to find the magic formula of the amount of time spent and proper environment cultivated to equate the "enough" of prayer—that "enough" of prayer that would ultimately get a response. Is it five continuous days of prayer? Three weeks of groggy, predawn prayer? Praying and crying? Praying and crying while lying on your stomach? Or is a simple whispered thought enough? Some offered that I'd hear God through fasting. Those who were athletic suggested I run in circles around my church sanctuary, belting out praise choruses. Finally, the typical and most popular recommendation was to repent. Obviously some mystical sin, or a bunch of them, had created a soundproof and everything-proof wall between me and God.

I compared my spirituality to that of my Christian friends, the ones who experienced daily prophetic words, divine dreams, constant peace, and fuzzy feelings. I became confused and irritated. I was not experiencing anything like that—just silence. I tried to seek God's voice through my own silent meditation but was met instead with the clanking sound of my dueling thoughts and feelings of fear.

I grabbed my Bible and played, with true sincerity and desperation, Russian biblical roulette. I closed my eyes, blindly flipped though the pages, and pointed my finger on a random passage, hoping I'd find a verse to magically and instantaneously evaporate the divine iron curtain. Much to my chagrin, my fingers would fall flat on verses such as "But yet in it shall be a tenth, and it shall return, and shall be eaten" (Isa. 6:13 KJV) or "I beseech thee for my son Onesimus, whom I have begotten in my bonds" (Philem. 1:10 KJV). Needless to say, they didn't help, or even make any sense to me, for that matter. I was still left to question the existence, activity, and love of a Savior who to me was nothing but silent. And I was trying, I really was.

When nothing worked, I felt like giving up. God seemed more like a phantom than my heavenly Father and more like a character out of *Grimm's Fairy Tales* than a Savior with scarred hands.

Whatever the situation we endure or however much our daily lives seem devoid of celestial verbiage, one of the most common knee-jerk reactions is to dart our eyes upward and question the intention and even existence of God. This is normal. Sometimes when we take that course of action, we still seem to receive no response and nothing that can provide some strain of emotional, spiritual, or mental relief. Does that mean there is no God? Does that mean he loves us any less? Does that mean God is the instigator of life's seemingly cruel and sick jokes at his own children's expense? No, but our faith alone can at its best leap, or otherwise stumble, over that unknown. And on my own journey, I learned a deeper faith was found where answers weren't readily available, where direction didn't necessarily exist, and where I had to believe and ultimately trust in what I couldn't see or feel. Through the road of my doubts, my wavering faith, and the course of writing this book, I had incredible opportunities to meet different people and listen to them share their stories with me. Some had been put through life's furnace and came out refined by the fuel of love. Others had turned their backs on God because they thought he had done the same first. Some were left with faint histories or scars of bitterness and desolation but somehow still radiate, to this day, a peace and a joy that cannot easily be explained.

I wrote this book for those people who are hurt, frustrated, depressed, angry, disappointed, or anxious because they can't see, feel, or hear God. Whether you stand questioning in the face of darkness or feel like you're serving a God who is on a permanent vacation, know he really is there. In spite of our fears and perception of his silence, his love, his grace, and his mercy remain. The hardest part is not losing our faith in the meantime.

My hope is that you, the reader, will come to experience a belief in a God who is and will forever remain faithful and continue believing, however hard it may be. My hope is that you will come out on the other side of questions, fears, and doubts with a simple faith that God was, is, and will always be there for you.

> I believe in the sun even when it is not shining.
> I believe in love even when feeling it not.
> I believe in God even when He is silent.
>
> Inscription on a cellar wall in Germany
> where Jews hid from Nazis

1

The Silent Treatment

My God, my God, why have you forsaken me?

Mark 15:34

If God accepted Christmas presents—and who knows, maybe he does—I would give him a bullhorn. And a microphone. And the most expensive, top-of-the-line Bose sound system with surround sound and award-winning Jewel Cube speakers. I'd give him a gift basket of everything related to sound so that maybe he would get the picture that I can't hear him and he needs to speak up. Now, I'm not a big fan of blaming God for stuff, so maybe the problem is me. Maybe I need to buy myself a holy hearing aid or something. But the fact of the matter remains that I've encountered enough bouts of silence from him in my life to come to the conclusion that he is, at times, silent.

Before you start arguing with my statement, let me say I do believe that we can hear God speak to us at certain times. He is capable of speaking in various ways, and we are just as capable of hearing. I believe these things are true. I believe he speaks in the still, small voice in our soul, through words of wisdom from other people, through the indescribable beauty of creation, and through the Bible. But that doesn't wash out his seasonal silence. The truth is, sometimes he doesn't say anything. This makes a lot of people feel uncomfortable and frustrated.

Who wants to surrender their very being to a God who is occasionally mute? Forget the fact that we don't physically see him. That's hard enough to accept. We can't see him beside us as we put the dishes away after the screamfest we had with our spouse during Sunday brunch. We can't see him next to us during the parent-teacher conference when we are told that our son has a learning disability and needs to go to a special school. We can't see him holding our hand when we're trying to do damage control after a particularly stupid mistake. This doesn't mean he's not there, of course. It just means that we have no sense of his tangibility to make us feel better or to give us a much-needed push as we walk in faith.

When I was a younger Christian, growing up in a very charismatic, black-and-white, legalistic Ukrainian denomination, I relied very much on signs and wonders to validate God's presence. He was as real as whatever funky, emotionally charged experience I had. Youth camps, retreats, and special services were an especially important component of my spirituality. For instance, every summer the young people from our church and our sister congregations would gather together for a week of fun and salvation. This was typically the week when everyone got saved, got resaved (for the fifth or fifteenth time), and offered God pie-in-the-sky promises of what they would do that year: "I will never ever say a curse word. I will hand out tracts at my high school and win at least one soul a week to Christ. I will spend every Friday and Saturday night volunteering at the local nursing home instead of going to parties. I will watch TBN instead of MTV. I will give up my dream of being an advertising executive and become a missionary to India." You get the idea.

The evening church services were packed with soaring emotions, tear-drenched prayers, and supernatural out-of-body experiences. Don't get me wrong. None of these things were wrong in and of themselves. I don't have a problem with a young person wanting to be a missionary or shedding a few (or a bunch of) tears during praise and worship. The problem I had—which I came to understand in my adult years—was that in our minds, the more outrageous your vows to God, the more goose pimples you felt, and the more hours you spent bawling your eyes dry, the more real God was or the more powerful your spiritual experience was. Also, the more of all of the above, the more God was inclined to surprise you with a life-changing speech sharing his wisdom, his thoughts, and his step-by-step plan for your life.

I did have my share of intense times at these events, but I never heard God speak to me as he apparently did to my friends. At some specific moments I did believe, in the bottom of my heart, that God communicated with me, but they weren't groundbreaking events. There was no lightning. No thunder. No wind. No earthquake. No fire. No shattering of crystal. The message was quiet, and it rested deep in my spirit. The words were few, the point was short, and the whole sentiment felt as light as a feather. I don't think I truly appreciated the magic of those moments, however, because I thought if God was God, he needed to make an appearance. A big and bold appearance, using a megaphone, of course.

His presence needed to be as loud and as unmistakable as Flavor Flav performing in *Swan Lake* at the Met wearing his signature clock necklace and a lacy, bubblegum pink tutu. I wouldn't (and shouldn't) have been able to miss God's grand entrance. Certainly I would not have been able to question whether or not he was real.

As I grew up and God continued to speak into the lives of the people around me with remarkable consistency (or so I was led to believe), telling them where to go to school, what career path to choose, what spouse to marry, and so on, I felt like a religious reject. In my own life, God was more silent than not. Granted, I'm sure there were times I didn't listen and other times when I should have been paying more attention. I won't be naive and deny that. Still, he just wasn't as transparent and as clear to see, hear, and understand as I believed he should have been.

Questions began to surface, and I, unfortunately, became obsessed with them. *Why is God ignoring me? What is wrong with me? What did I do or not do? Am I not doing enough? Does God hate me? Am I not being sincere? Should I pray more? Should I fast more? Should I go to church more? Should I slice my wrists and turn myself into a literal sacrifice for him?* I allowed them to mold the image I had of God into a really ugly shape and distort the beauty of faith.

I've since resolved, or at least come to have more peace than not with the fact, that God doesn't communicate with me in theatrics but with a quiet assurance. Sure, it bothers me every now and then, but I remind myself that it just happens to be his modus operandi. It's okay if I beg God to reveal himself to me in a dream and all I dream about is sitting in high school algebra class with nothing but a pair of roller skates on. It's okay if God doesn't respond to my questions in an audible voice that sounds like Morgan Freeman's in

Bruce Almighty. I don't have to walk around thinking I'm a terrible person because other people are hearing God talk to them in flowery soliloquies that could match the length of a novella and I'm not. It's okay. It's simply okay.

Our faith journey will not be loaded with hourly dialogue with the Almighty. For the most part, spirituality looks more like a deep trust (sometimes serene, sometimes frantic) than a dramatic overture played by a full-size orchestra. Being Christlike is not about finding God or seeing God show up only in the organized chaos of supernatural experiences. He is not an active part of your life just because you may have more ethereal moments than the marketing director from your small group. God is real if you act like a holy roller on fire or if you are a faith-filled but tired and with no time to spare stay-at-home mom doing a thousand things at once.

At some particular moments God's silence is more distressing—at the tragic times when terrible circumstances occur that force you to view your life in two segments: before the calamity and after. It's when people say things like "before my daughter died," "after I got cancer," "before my husband left me," and "after I filed for bankruptcy." Not only does God seem to have crazy-glued his trap shut during these times, but he is nowhere to be found. He is silent and he is hidden.

God on the Sidelines

The book of Job is about a man of the same name, a very successful family and business man who could have probably written a *New York Times* best-selling book about how to be great at everything. God is in heaven, beaming with joy because Job is still a righteous man in spite of his great wealth. Job's riches haven't quite gone to his head in a prideful manner. He is humble, he is kind, and he is generous. Satan comes around one day and strikes up a conversation with God. God starts bragging about his golden boy Job, and every complimentary word God utters about the guy makes Satan's slimy skin crawl. So he decides to up the conversation a notch and play a little Russian roulette with the apparent "man of God."

See, the devil is a very smart guy. He knows how easy it is to sing "Oh, how I love Jesus" when life is pretty much carefree. And he knows that when life goes topsy-turvy, the natural, human tendency is to run away from God after we've shaken our fists in his invisible face, told him how disgustingly cruel he is, and damned him out of our lives. In his sneaky and inimitable way, Satan boldly tells God something like this: "I'll bet you a hundred bucks that as soon as bad stuff starts happening to Job, the first thing he's gonna do is curse you. Then he'll curse his sorry you-know-what for having thought that he would get a good life by serving you." Satan is as confident as a champion poker player and looks God dead in the eye when he speaks. God, ever the calm, cool, and collected Creator of the universe, rolls his eyes at this cocky son of a gun and replies, "Go right ahead and do what you need to do. I know Job's character and I know his heart." God is not moved in the least by Satan's wager.

Satan then goes ballistic and starts making terrible things happen in Job's life. He convinces a thug to steal all of Job's oxen and donkeys. He sends a fire down to burn up Job's sheep. Then he adds a little fuel to the proverbial fire and causes a tornado-like wind to come and destroy the house Job's kids are in; all ten of them die. Finally, Satan strikes Job with wicked and grotesque boils that cover his entire body. The pain and the itching are so bad that Job spends most of his days scratching himself raw with a broken piece of pottery.

Most of the book of Job details his complaints, frustrations, rage, and confusion about the situation. He yells at God. He verbally battles with his friends, who of course are quick and eager to put in their two cents about the whole thing. Job is getting no answers from God for the sudden catastrophes. No explanations. No reasons. Not even an "I'm here and I've got your back" from God. I imagine Job's cries pierce and echo throughout heaven. His words are powerful and hard to ignore.

In his eighth speech, which was directed to one of his friends in particular, Job complains that God is absent. Job has been abandoned. He's looking left and right for God and comes up empty-handed each time. He can't even find a faint trace of his Maker. Nothing. Zilch. Zero. Nada. *The Message* puts it this way: "I travel East looking for him—I find no one; then West, but not a trace; I go North, but he's hidden his tracks; then South, but not even a glimpse" (Job 23:8–9).

Isn't that how we all feel when we've been sucker punched by life tragedies? We want God to arrive on the scene of our calamities with a magic wand to either make the undesirable disappear or make it all better. Or we want him to reconcile our pains and misfortune with some meaningful verbiage that will justify what is happening to us. But what do we experience most times? Nothing. Silence. God seems to be sitting on the sidelines of our disaster, not even cheering us on but eating an overstuffed hot dog and asking the vendor where the porta-potty is. Or it seems he is more concerned with Joe Schmoe's situation since he prays more than we do and never has a lusty thought cross his pure mind. *Seems* is the operative word, of course. The reality is that God has not disappeared. Nor is he a sadistic being who delights in watching us squirm and protest when we are pummeled by stinky situations. He just isn't doing or saying what we want or hope he will do or say.

The Jewish people who were waiting for the Messiah to return went through something similar. For hundreds of years, the nation of Israel was hoping to have their Davidic kingdom restored. They were waiting for a deliverer, a warrior, to radically and powerfully redeem them from oppression. They were hoping for a leader with a sword to "proclaim . . . the day of vengeance of . . . God" (Isa. 61:2 KJV). They wanted a heavenly Rambo to come down, wipe out their enemies, and give them back the glories of their kingdom.

What they got was Jesus. The Son of God, but a flesh and bones, human baby boy who was born in a dirty and smelly stable. They got a carpenter who was humble and meek. They got a teacher who came to bring peace, not provoke the fight of the ages. They got the suffering servant, as Isaiah prophesied. What they didn't get, which was what they wanted, was the Arnold Schwarzenegger character in the movie *Commando*. Jesus's style of fulfilling his mission in this world was a disappointment to many. He basically let the air out of their inflated tires of hope and rescue. He didn't come with guns blazing. He came with kindness and with a message of hope.

Before he stepped into the spotlight and revealed who he really was, Jesus kept a low profile and made it crystal clear to his entourage, who were witnesses to his supernatural feats and miracles, not to spread the word of who he was. It frustrated them to no end. "Leave here and go to Judea," one of them said, "where your followers can see your miracles! You can't become famous if you hide like this! If you can do such wonderful things, show yourself to the world!" (John 7:3–4). But revelation wasn't part of Jesus's plan just yet, and he simply responded, "Now is not the right time for me" (John 7:6). What did Jesus's followers want him to do?

Make a public spectacle out of himself so everyone would know that he was the Messiah, that he was the Chosen One, that he would save them, and that he was the man everyone had been waiting for.

When Jesus did have his "induction ceremony," it was without the pomp and circumstance most would have expected. You would think he would have held the event in a palace, dressed in royal robes, and been flanked on all sides by a team of bodyguards with high-tech earpieces and Armani suits. But it was nothing like that. Jesus rode through Jerusalem on a donkey—a simple, ordinary, flat gray–colored donkey. As he sat on the braying, sluggish animal, he shouted, "Don't be afraid, people of Jerusalem. Look, your King is coming, riding on a donkey's colt" (John 12:15). Not exactly the triumphant entry of a king.

Many of the folks who were waiting for the arrival of their Messiah wanted a warrior. They got something different. Different, but better. Different, but divine. Different, but necessary. God wouldn't have had it any other way. In the same vein, we don't want a hidden or silent God. We want Santa Claus. We want Houdini. We want Superman. We want a God who will get into the thick of things with us and immediately clean up our messes and pluck all of the bad events out of our otherwise good lives.

In this fallen world, while God doesn't really sit on the sidelines thumbing through the funny pages and checking out our moves on the playing field of life every five minutes, he does allow life to run its course. Sure, it can be quite an ugly and treacherous course sometimes, but God's presence is with us. He is with us. And he doesn't have to do magic tricks or orchestrate the miraculous to prove his existence, his care, or his love for us. Many of us have a hard time accepting that truth.

The Gallows of Life

In his book *Night*, prolific writer Elie Wiesel recounts his experience as a survivor in the concentration camps during the Holocaust. At one point he describes the public execution of a young boy. The boy met death while hanging mercilessly on a swinging rope in front of a wide-eyed audience of emaciated men three times his age. In Wiesel's own words:

> So he remained for more than half an hour, lingering between life and death, writhing before our eyes. And we were forced to look at him at close range. He was still alive when I passed him. His tongue was still red, his eyes not yet extinguished.
>
> Behind me, I heard the . . . man asking, "For God's sake, where is God?"
>
> And from within me, I heard a voice answer, "Where is He? This is where—hanging from this gallows."[1]

It was a nightmare just to have the rest of the world stand silent and inactive while eleven million innocent people, mostly Jews, were killed as a result of the command of a ruthless dictator, Adolf Hitler. It was an even worse nightmare not to have God intervene when hell literally broke loose across eastern Europe. Many people have reconciled the Holocaust with their faith in God, and many others have not. Professor Emil Ludwig Fackenheim, a noted Jewish philosopher, Reform rabbi, and Holocaust survivor, made it very clear through his writing of the "614th commandment" that a belief in God after such a catastrophic event is possible and should even be pursued:

> If the 614th commandment is binding upon the authentic Jew, then we are, first, commanded to survive as Jews, lest the Jewish people perish. We are commanded, second, to remember in our very guts and bones the martyrs of the Ho-

locaust, lest their memory perish. *We are forbidden, thirdly, to deny or despair of God, however much we may have to contend with him or with belief in him, lest Judaism perish.* We are forbidden, finally, to despair of the world as the place which is to become the kingdom of God, lest we help make it a meaningless place in which God is dead or irrelevant and everything is permitted. To abandon any of these imperatives, in response to Hitler's victory at Auschwitz, would be to hand him yet other, posthumous victories.[2]

On the contrary, Rabbi Richard Rubenstein developed the "death of God" theory after the Holocaust. He believed it was impossible to believe in God and wrote, "As children of the Earth, we are undeceived concerning our destiny. We have lost all hope, consolation and illusion."[3] When God's presence isn't apparent, it can lead to a pretty hopeless situation and, ultimately, a pretty hopeless people.

History is bursting with instances of tragedies coupled with the same type of questions that were asked during the Holocaust. Where was God during the genocide in Rwanda? Where was God on 9/11? Where was God during Hurricane Katrina? Where was God during the 2008 earthquake in China? Where was God (fill in the blank)? Why doesn't he do anything? Why doesn't he say anything? Why doesn't he intervene? Etcetera, etcetera, etcetera. Sometimes those questions are best met with silence, because certainly no reasons or excuses can ever be good enough to justify the horrific.

God hung on the gallows, Wiesel writes, and certainly in our own lives we've got our own gallows that sway in the not-so-distant horizon. The gallows of a marriage gone completely wrong. The gallows of watching your child fight for her life in a pediatric burn unit. The gallows of sexual abuse. The gallows of injustice. The gallows of depression. The gallows of death. I do believe God's presence is in the gallows, but not as a dying holy figure who doesn't care and who disappears into oblivion when the going gets tough. God is on the gallows of life by our side. He allows us to go through things we'd rather not go through and provides us with comfort, peace, and assurance in that meantime.

In his book *Discerning the Way*, Paul M. Van Buren writes:

> It is therefore not out of order, if extremely hard to say, that God must have been present in the ovens of the death camps and in the mass graves of Eastern Europe. Where else could He have been than there precisely where His beloved sons and daughters were being tortured and slaughtered? The God of the philosophers may have withdrawn. The God of Golgotha—who is no other than the God of Abraham, Isaac and Jacob—would have had to be there.[4]

True, this may be hard to swallow for anyone, let alone people who have experienced the unimaginable, but what other choice is there? Believing God is a sadist who is hidden and silent on purpose to get his kicks? God doesn't impose himself on us. He doesn't even pressure us to believe. But one thing is for certain: he gives us the choice, and it is completely up to us whether to keep believing in him or not, whatever may happen in our lives.

Responding to God's Silent Treatment

When we stand questioning in the presence of the Silent One, the empty feeling in our spirit from his unresponsiveness does not reflect his actual absence. It may mean the extent of our anxieties and the drowning force of our circumstances are too overwhelming for clarity to step in. It may mean, though it is impossible to comprehend, that silence is better than any visual or verbal response of hope. It may mean that God has to allow human beings and nature to be just that: human beings and nature, not robots or robotic forces that he controls like puppets on a string. It may mean . . . who knows? How are we ever supposed to figure it out?

Through the moments when God seems silent or absent, we are given choices: to keep believing in him full steam ahead; to abandon the whole God thing in its entirety; or to trust him sometimes kicking and screaming, sometimes with a needy desperation, and sometimes somewhere in between. Job did the latter. You wouldn't think so if you read through the book of Job, though. Many people who are not entirely familiar with this biblical text assume that it is filled with detailed story after detailed story of Job's troubles. But it's not really just a book about suffering. It's the recording of the many speeches given by a man who doesn't stop talking about or to God. It's about a man who doesn't give up his quest to find answers. It's about a man who doesn't abandon the idea that God could and would, someday and somehow, respond to his endless, tear-filled tirades.

Job whines and complains and cries and argues and gets angry at the God who seems to be snubbing him. He hates the silence that is coming from the Being who once blessed him beyond measure, but he doesn't use it as ammunition to turn away from God. Job never throws up his hands in frustration and says, "Look here, God, or whatever you say your name is. I'm in a bind. You've taken everything away from me. I can't even have a decent night's sleep because my flesh is practically eating me alive. You're not doing anything about it. You're not even giving me wisdom about the situation. This must mean you don't exist. Well, since that's probably the case, sayonara, buddy. Take all the blessing crap and shove it where the sun don't shine. I'm outta here."

No, Job keeps running his mouth to God, to his friends, to himself, to his wife, to whoever will listen, really. He especially keeps pleading his case before God. Never mind the mile-long list of grievances that colors his prayers or that he constantly questions the character and motives of God. What's important to remember is that Job never stops talking to God. He never stops looking up. That in itself is a sign, however faint, that hope is still present. It flutters inside Job's pained heart like a baby dove with a broken wing. Job believes, in his own honest way, that God will eventually do something. Exactly what? Who knows? But his confidence in God never leaves him, though it seems microscopic on some days.

In one particular conversation, a religious lightbulb illuminates in Job's friend Bildad's head. He believes he received divine wisdom he ought to share with scab-encrusted Job. Bildad tells Job that he is a wicked man and that his suffering is being caused because he has obviously done something very bad. Bildad practically chews Job out and enumerates the terrible things that happen to wicked people. "Shame on you!" Bildad says.

Job retorts with a biting monologue of what a bad friend Bildad is. His eyes are probably brimming with tears as he questions why Bildad's words clearly serve to totally demoralize and crush Job. Then Job says something quite profound. After he begs Bildad for a smidgen of pity and sympathy, Job's spirit turns an interesting corner. "Still," Job cries, "I know that God lives—the One who gives me back my life" (Job 19:25 Message). Other translations mark Job's words as, "I know my Redeemer (or Defender) lives." Therein lies the crux of Job's faith. In an earlier dialogue Job had declared a similar sentiment: "Though he [God] slay me, yet I will hope in him" (Job 13:15 NIV). The bottom line? Job has not given up his faith in God.

God does, of course, finally respond to Job's question. While it isn't the reply Job was hoping for, it serves its purpose and quickly shuts Job up. God reminds his servant of the sovereignty of God, of the complexity of the world and the creatures who inhabit it, of the intricate and unimaginable details with which God rules the world. He puts Job in his place by saying something like, "You think you can do my job? Good luck." My favorite part, though, is when God condemns Job's friends. During this entire time they had repeatedly told him such things as: "You're doing this and that wrong." "This is happening to you because of such-and-such." "Try doing this and it'll be better." "You are a bad person and are just reaping the dirty and nasty things you have surely sown." It seemed Job's friends had every answer in the book for Job's troubles, but none of their advice or commentary gave him any interim comfort. It just made him more miserable. I suppose it's easy to be a know-it-all when you stand outside the circle of someone's tragedy.

Let this serve as a warning to you. When someone you know is going through something terrible and they are questioning God's silence and absence, don't be so quick to run your mouth and give them some judgmental explanation, in your oh-so-infinite wisdom, of what's really going on in their spiritual life. Sure, you might be right (maybe), but the truth is, you don't know for sure why things happen. All you should really do is pray for them. And love them. And give them the grace to experience the situation however they need to experience it.

When God seems absent . . . when he is not saying a word . . . when dark silence collides with your questions, your prayers, and even your faith, don't stop believing in him. Yell at him, complain until your lips turn blue, flip through the Bible like a maniac for some answers, do whatever you

31

have to do—just don't give up. You may not get your answers, and your circumstances might not go away, but he'll do something to give you the peace and the grace to keep moving forward.

———•———

Horatio Spafford had a loving wife and five adorable children and made a substantial living as a prominent attorney. He was a pillar of and heavily involved in the community where he lived in Chicago. The year 1871 turned out to be a horrible year for him and his family. His four-year-old son died of scarlet fever, and as he and his wife were nursing their tender wounds, just a short while later the great Chicago Fire destroyed practically everything they owned.

A religious man, Horatio kept his faith and did the best he could to make the most of his life in light of those two terrible events. Two years later, in November of 1873, he decided his family needed some rest and relaxation, and he planned a trip to Europe to relieve a little stress. Horatio sent his wife and four girls ahead of him, as he needed to tie up a number of loose ends concerning his business. He wanted to, after all, enjoy the holiday without worrying about what needed to get done at the office. He waved good-bye to the women in his life and watched as the ship sailed off. He would meet up with them in England in a week or so.

Two days later, Horatio received a cable from his wife. It read, "Saved alone." The ship that had carried his wife and four daughters had been struck by another vessel and, in only a few minutes, sank deep into the ocean. Two hundred and twenty-six people lost their lives in that accident, including his four little girls. Where was God? Hadn't this man suffered enough? Why was God on the sidelines? Why didn't he do anything? Were his hands tied?

A few days after hearing of the death of all of his daughters, Horatio left Chicago and took off for England on a ship to meet his wife. I cannot even imagine the thoughts and emotions stirring in his heart during the days he spent crossing the Atlantic Ocean. Maybe he was numb with shock. Perhaps he was stilled in his spirit, overwhelmed by the injustice of the succession of tragedies he endured. At one point during his journey, the captain of the ship, knowing about Horatio's recent loss, beckoned him on deck. The man pointed out a particular spot in the swirling blue sea that glistened like sapphire diamonds. As the waves gently slapped the sides of the ship and the salt water wafted gloriously in the air, the captain somberly showed Horatio the place where his daughters had drowned.

You can imagine how his heart must have sank as he furiously wiped away the hot tears that flooded his face. Four girls. Four innocent, beautiful girls dead in an instant. What Horatio did next is fascinating. I don't know if I could do it. Frankly, you probably don't know if you could do it. But something was grounded in the very core of his spirit that allowed him—in nothing short of a miraculous way—to write a song, one of my favorite hymns, titled "It Is Well with My Soul." He penned lyrics that spoke of a firm faith. A quiet assurance. A soft trust in God even in spite of his seeming absence and events that simply should not have been.

> When peace like a river attendeth my way,
> When sorrows like sea billows roll;
> Whatever my lot, Thou hast caused me to say,
> "It is well, it is well with my soul." . . .
>
> Though Satan should buffet, though trials should
>   come,
> Let this blest assurance control,

That Christ has regarded my helpless estate,
And hath shed His own blood for my soul.

It is well with my soul,
It is well, it is well with my soul.

Imagine that. Scribbling thoughts about the condition of his soul through those sea billows that had swallowed up his daughters. Horatio could have forgotten God. He could have cursed God. He could have given up. He could have allowed grief to destroy his hope. He could have done all those things quite easily, and it wouldn't have taken that much effort. Honestly, who would have blamed the poor guy?

But through the unexplained tragedies, through the seeming absence of God, through the blinding tears, through the bottomless sorrow, it was well with his soul. I don't mention this story to minimize our own personal tragedies or compare our seemingly insignificant questions about God's presence with Horatio's situation, but it would do us all well to meditate on it.

Things happen. Crazy things. Terrible things. Inexplicable things. Unfair things. While our immediate reaction is not always entirely kosher, these things are what they are. It's okay to initially react by yelling, screaming, crying, getting mad, and even avoiding God, because we're not sure what to say. But there comes a point when we have to get back into the nesting place of our spirituality. We can continue in relationship with God, believing he is still with us regardless of what happens and how we feel, or we can believe that his silence or lack of intervention means that God is an apathetic or twisted, pathetic, and sinister being. In his book *A Room Called Remember*, Frederick Buechner writes how an indication of our deep love for God is continuing to love him in the moments when we are paralyzed by fear that he doesn't love us or, worse, that he isn't even real at all.

God can be silent. God can be hidden. God can be quite difficult to figure out. It's pretty important to our well-being that we trust him especially in these moments. I know it's not the easiest thing in the world to do. I know it can seem too much to ask. And I know it will call for some pain, questions, and wonder. But know this: that kind of belief in God will produce in your spirit the kind of spiritual bedrock that, though it may endure its fair share of cracks and fissures, will never crumble to dust.

2

Begging for a Miracle

To me every hour of the light and dark is a miracle,
every cubic inch of space is a miracle.

Walt Whitman

I can still feel the creepy silence that invaded our home the night my father died. I sat on the floor of my sister's bedroom, my face pressed against the glass of the window that exposed the glorious view of the Manhattan skyline. If I looked hard enough, I could see a blinking red light on top of the Empire State Building. Nobody else was home. It was just me, a fourteen-year-old, wide-eyed, panicky girl clutching a laminated three-by-three poem titled "Miracles" to my chest. I don't remember exactly what the poem said. I just remember it talked about how God performed miracles, and how it was our duty to believe in them, and how nothing was impossible for him to do.

I was waiting for my miracle in the form of a phone call from the hospital saying that the doctors managed to revive my father and that he was alive and well. I was waiting for my miracle of discovering that his dramatic "dying" episode was nothing but a false alarm or a hard-hitting reminder from God that we should never take life, or people for that matter, lightly. I was waiting for the miracle of my father bursting through our huge wooden doors, grabbing me in his muscular arms, and saying in Ukrainian with a playful wink, "What's the matter with you? Stop crying! Look at me, I'm here. I'm alive."

I never got my miracle.

It was a cold Sunday night when my dad went to bed really early complaining of severe abdominal pain, a migraine, and feeling exhausted. These weren't out of the ordinary symptoms. He always had headaches, and because he worked so hard, it was normal for him to be so tired. The abdominal pain? It was probably just stress related.

My father had gone to church that night with my sister Vivien. Ten years later, I was at the home of a woman named Joy who happened to be at that church service, and she shared something with me that rekindled the memory. She and I were talking about the tragedy of untimely and sudden deaths, when out of nowhere tears began to roll down her face. She started to describe that night at church with such intricate details you would have thought it happened yesterday.

Joy told me my sister played the harp and, as expected, played beautifully. For no particular reason, Joy looked at my dad, who she noticed was beaming with pride. Then Joy said, "I can't explain it, A. J., but your dad looked like he was glowing. I remember thinking he looked like an angel or that he was in heaven. He had this peaceful and illuminating presence about him that I still can't describe except to say it was heavenlike."

Well, not but two hours after church, my father lay under the covers in his king-size bed with the lights turned off. He was dying, but nobody in our family knew it just yet. A few minutes before an aortic aneurysm ruptured in his body without any warning, he called out to me. It was more like a faint moan. I was in my bedroom next to his and just barely heard him. I remember not wanting to go in his room, but I had no legitimate reason for my hesitation.

When I got to his bedside, he looked terrible. Exhausted. Burned-out. Run down. Worst of all, he looked like he was in extreme pain, which of course he was. He asked me to pray for him because he didn't feel good. I prayed, but I was very much embarrassed doing so. I hated praying out loud (and still do). I wondered what good the prayer of a naive, immature, and awkward fourteen-year-old would do. What would I say? Would it even matter? Would my words make my dad feel better? What if my prayer sounded stupid, and he regretted even asking me to pray for him?

But I prayed. About three seconds into my pathetic "Dear-Lord-help-uh-Jesus-uh-please . . ." stuttering prayer, I felt like something big and powerful kicked me in the gut. It was a haunting feeling that had the weight of concrete. In that moment, I knew beyond a shadow of a doubt that something was seriously wrong with my dad. The more alarmed I felt, the more my words grew stronger and more faith-filled. I asked for God to heal my dad of whatever he was suffering from. I asked God to take all of my dad's pain away. I asked God for my dad to be better and be able to go to work the next day and all the days after that. I asked God to let my father be my father forever. I left the room after he warmly thanked me and kissed me on the cheek for the last time. Only moments later he started to internally bleed to death. Nobody saw it coming. He'd had a physical exam a few months earlier, and the doctor had remarked about how healthy he was.

A few minutes before our familial doomsday, I ran out of his bedroom to the downstairs bathroom and hurled myself into the corner of the room. I hunched down into a fetal position on the cold, marble floor and listened to my heart pound in my chest. It was beating a hundred beats per second, and I could barely breathe. I sobbed like a newborn baby, and this time I didn't care how articulate I sounded. I begged God to save my daddy's life. I screamed. I cried. I furiously pummeled the hard floor with my fists. My shoulders shook from the heaving sobs. I did whatever I could do, in my own knowledge and power, to grab God's attention and force his miraculous powers to extend toward my father's ailing body. In my heart I knew God was the God of the impossible. He could do anything. And that meant he could heal my dad. I had faith. I believed. Nobody or nothing could tell me something different.

Ten minutes later, chaos broke out. Or maybe hell is a better word. My mom was in hysterics, wailing at maximum volume for someone to call 911. I heard the frantic pace of my sister's footsteps as she (an army medical specialist at the time) hightailed it to Dad's bedroom to perform ultimately unsuccessful CPR. My older brother tried to keep my mother as calm as possible. I jetted out of my porcelain prayer closet to find my youngest brother and shield his little self from the madness.

Before the ambulance arrived, twelve minutes of pandemonium ensued. Two of my siblings and my mother hovered over my dad, who was violently gasping for breath that just wouldn't come. The sound was horrific, and his belly was beginning to bloat up in a grotesque, disfiguring shape. I peeked at the scene from the doorway and quickly turned away after seeing my sister pound his chest with her delicate hands to no avail and hearing my mom's powerful shrieks of lament as she practically scratched at her body and the air in grief. It was too much to take.

Finally, somber-faced medical personnel swarmed our house with a scary-looking heart defibrillator, liquid-filled plastic bags, needles, and a cold, hard stretcher. The walkie-talkies hooked on their pants blurted out random beeps and urgent messages that reminded me of an episode of *Rescue 911*, which, ironically, our whole family used to watch together. I heard them hectically working on my dad to revive him, but there was no point. The bleeding was too bad.

I watched them trying to strategically maneuver the stretcher with my dad's limp body strapped onto it down our winding staircase. Two minutes later I was sitting in my sister's bedroom, listening to my little brother snoring on her bed in la-la land. From her window I watched the ambulance whiz down our street, leaving behind an echo of the screaming sirens. My mom and siblings followed behind in the family car. I was stunned. The grim reaper had knocked on our door. It felt like not only had God invited him in, but God pulled out all the stops for Death. God had the guest room fixed up for him and a plate of warm cookies and milk waiting in the kitchen.

Death has a way of coating your heart with shock. It's a numbing veil necessary for survival or maintaining a sense of sanity. I reread that "Miracles" poem over and over, repeating the same prayers for God not to let my father die, even though he had probably been pronounced dead by that point. But I still believed. I tell you, the amount of faith I had was extraordinary. Maybe it was a powerful hope combined with a numbing disbelief of the reality of death at hand, but I refused to give up believing that God would do something miraculous. Hey, that's what the poem said.

What was the answer to my prayers? A funeral.

The service was a surreal experience. The funeral home was packed with many family members, church folks, friends of the family, people my dad knew but we didn't, and neighbors from the community. About half of the guests had to stand the entire service because there weren't enough chairs. The guest of honor was my dad, who lay peacefully in a simple wooden coffin, which was indicative of the simplicity of his soul. I put my hand on his arm. I touched his face. I think I may even have poked his belly. His skin was waxy and gray, and his body was ice cold and as hard as a rock. The physical contact with the lifeless mass of bones and flesh made death real. My father wasn't coming back.

I became confused and angry, especially when I saw my little brother prancing around the funeral parlor. He was only four. What would he do? How well would he fare without a male figure in the home? And what about my mom? She had to raise four kids on her own with a nearly depleted bank account. What would she do? What were any of us going to do?

I don't know who decided on the program for the service, but one of the songs that was picked out was an old hymn called "Leaning on the Everlasting Arms." I thought that was a dumb choice. Leaning on exactly whose arms? The arms of a God who didn't do anything about my prayers? The arms of a God who maybe never heard my cries to begin with? The arms of a God who just maybe didn't even exist?

To be honest, I was numb for a while, and my life was turned so upside down that I couldn't focus on grieving, only on surviving. Many sections of my teenage years I really don't even remember. I know the rest of my family shared similar experiences. But even through the tough exterior and the walls I'm sure we all put up—the coats of armor we wore so we would be fine no matter what—I had to come to terms with a God who didn't perform every miracle. A God who didn't answer every prayer. A God who let terrible things happen and didn't offer an explanation as to why. I had to learn to lean on God's everlasting arms in light of the fact that, or perhaps especially because, at times, life is just not fair.

Maybe the miracle was that even in the face of death, even in the shadow of the grim reaper's scythe dangling in the distance, arms even stronger than my dad's were available to hold and carry me. Now, that truth didn't ease the pain of prematurely losing a parent. It didn't shoo away the emptiness in my heart. Nor did the assurance that God is present, even when things don't go my way, make me want to do the Macarena and pretend life is great all the time. But I did feel his arms wrapped around me. Not in a physical way, but in my spirit. And it did give me a spiritual edge for other heartbreaking experiences in the future when I prayed so hard and so furiously for things I didn't wind up getting. I think about his everlasting arms when I'm alone, when I'm afraid, and when I'm in a bind. When I'm faced with the unknown, maybe not immediately, but I always end up resting in the truth that his arms are there for me like a mother hen who shields her chicks under her feathered wings. "The eternal God is your refuge, and his everlasting arms are under you" (Deut. 33:27).

One of the writers of the song "Leaning on the Everlasting Arms" penned the lyrics after he got word that the wives of two of his friends had passed away. I'll be the first to say that death is a real ugly thing to experience for the loved ones who are left behind. It's cold, dark, barren, and lonely. It's a haunting place for many different reasons. It's painful. No words of comfort suffice in the moments when death takes the place of a miracle. Sure, it's hard to justify a good God in the presence of the bad. And it's easy to disbelieve God's goodness, let alone his existence. But in these moments, sometimes it's best to give up relying on your own equilibrium in life and lean on God instead.

Don't think just because your miracle never came that you didn't pray enough, didn't believe enough, or are not good enough. It simply means that your miracle didn't come and you are not the architect of the blueprint of your life, or anyone else's for that matter. Don't quit believing; just lean a little more on God's arms.

> What a fellowship, what a joy divine,
> Leaning on the everlasting arms;
> What a blessedness, what a peace is mine,
> Leaning on the everlasting arms.
>
> Leaning, leaning, safe and secure from all alarms;
> Leaning, leaning, leaning on the everlasting arms.
>
> What have I to dread, what have I to fear,
> Leaning on the everlasting arms?
> I have blessed peace with my Lord so near,
> Leaning on the everlasting arms.

The Problem of Signs, Wonders, Quick Fixes, and Cure-alls

It is impossible not to equate a supernatural God with supernatural feats. If you a live a spiritual life, you open up yourself to a realm of possibility where strange things occur that are beyond reasonable explanation. People of faith believe for certain things that actually happen. Malignant tumors that showed up on X-rays one day disappear from the same patient's body the next day. Financial dilemmas that called for the signing of bankruptcy papers are torn up because a hefty check came in the mail at the last minute. Women who were never able to conceive because of severe medical problems start shedding tears of joy at the positive line on a pregnancy test.

Some folks have "lesser scale" miracles that are still, in their minds, just as big and grand as "bigger scale" miracles. A man who has been single for forty-five years finally meets the woman of his dreams. A medical student gets her first choice for where she can conduct her residency. A professor working twenty years on a project finally gets a grant he's been waiting for. I could go on and on. I'm sure you have some stories of your own or of people you know who have experienced a miracle or two.

I absolutely believe in miracles. I believe positive things can happen that are beyond our wildest dreams and beyond the realm of reality. I know that God does wonders and heals people and changes their hearts. He does all kinds of great things. I have no doubt in my mind that God can and does perform the miraculous. However, I've come to see the damage that comes when people rely on miracles for their faith, when people refuse to believe in or acknowledge God until he repeats the Red Sea phenomenon and parts the Atlantic Ocean, or when people abandon their faith because their prayers and faith did not produce a miracle and so, they say, obviously the spiritual life doesn't work. Frederick Buechner writes, "Faith in God is less apt to proceed from miracles than miracles from faith in God."[1]

"Show up, God," we yell on earth, staring at a crystal blue sky that stretches to infinity. "Show yourself and I'll believe. Show yourself and I'll keep on believing. Do X, Y, or Z and

I'll put my trust in you." Nothing is wrong with asking God for something with the right motives. The problem lies when our intentions are warped and we would rather God act as a spiritual Santa Claus than an all-powerful being we can't quite figure out. We don't want to pray, "Your will be done"; we want to name and claim things.

This reminds me of what C. S. Lewis wrote about his prayers begging God to heal his dying mother. "I had approached God, or my idea of God, without love, without awe, even without fear. He was, in my mental picture of this miracle, to appear neither as Savior nor as Judge, but merely as a magician; and when He had done what was required of Him I supposed He would simply—well, go away. It never crossed my mind that the tremendous contact which I solicited should have any consequences beyond restoring the status quo."[2]

I have a problem with fad diets. Granted, I've been on many of them, including the famous Master Cleanse one where I lost ten pounds in five days. I gained the weight back the minute I bit into a piece of whole wheat bread, but I did get a few days of skinny glory under my belt. Try telling someone the best way to lose weight is to exercise and eat less. "Don't stuff the second slice of pizza in your mouth, and walk around the block for an hour." "Trade that Krispy Kreme for a Granny Smith apple." "Try biking to the library instead of driving the three miles."

Who wants to hear or do that? Less food and more activity are B-O-R-I-N-G. And it takes too long. So we, especially Americans, spend billions of dollars on "as seen on TV" products that guarantee us thinner thighs in a week. Or we load our vitamin drawers with bottles of fat-burning, carb-reducing pills that promise us we will still lose weight even if we eat chocolate and drink beer all day. Or we slap on a fancy, gooey cream that costs us three hundred dollars a dollop and rub it into our cellulite-ridden thighs because we are sure to see results in three minutes or our money back. What's wrong with us? We want the quick fix. We want the answer without studying the problem. We want the diploma without attending a class. We want everything proven without closing our eyes and taking a leap (or even a tiny step) forward to ignite our faith. We want signs. We want wonders. And we want them now. We do spirituality, as a whole, a great disservice by begging for miracles to validate our faith or move us forward on the journey.

When Jesus walked on this earth, he performed many miracles. He turned water into wine. He healed the lame, the blind, and the deaf. He made a feast out of a few measly scraps of fish and bread. He cured diseases like leprosy. The Gospels record some instances where Jesus was approached by the religious leaders of the day, who demanded from him a sign to prove his true identity. They frequently did or said things to try to push his buttons because Jesus stood so far out of the religious compass they lived by. They were eager to trap him somehow because he was so different from them. They waited for him to say or do something so they could jump down his throat, tag him as a heretic, and destroy his so-called ministry. In different ways, they asked him, "Why do you do this? Doesn't the Law require you to do that instead?" They never gave him the benefit of the doubt and never once believed even a tiny bit that perhaps he was the prophesied Messiah. No, Jesus was different, much too different from them for him to be associated as a man of God, or even a prophet or a reputable teacher. They pinned Jesus as a zealot who rocked the boat on purpose to get on their last nerves. He was a fraud, they thought, a liar, and a fool.

One day these holy rollers "went to Jesus and began to argue with him. They tested him by demanding that he perform a miraculous sign from heaven. With a deep sigh he asked, "Why do these people demand a sign? I can guarantee this truth: If these people are given a sign, it will be far different than what they want!" Then he left them there" (Mark 8:11–13 GOD'S WORD). Jesus hated the demands that were placed on him to perform signs and wonders and miracles instead of asking him for forgiveness, for peace, for love, for more faith, for joy, or for contentment. It seems the latter things were just as exciting then as it is today to lose only a pound or two a week based on eating less and exercising more or to get a job instead of gambling or playing the lottery in hopes of gaining financial security.

The Pharisees didn't want to be touched on a deep, internal level to challenge or strengthen their spirituality; they simply wanted proof. They wanted Jesus to make a scene using the supernatural. Each time he refused, rolling his eyes and shaking his head at the ignorance and the impure intentions of these leaders. Don't get me wrong. I am not juxtaposing our sincere prayers for miracles or other things with the self-satisfying demands of those pious religious leaders. We all have needs that are bigger than ourselves that require God's intervention. But these guys were basically making fun of Jesus and asking him to do things just so they could get a perverse kick out of it.

Some of us define God's power, his love for us, and even his existence based on how many answers to prayers we get, how things in life go our way, and how many miracles speckle our faith walk. Others demand things of God from a spiteful heart, almost for a reassurance that he won't do particular things so they can smugly say they were right and he doesn't exist. Sometimes these things can happen with naive Christians not so much because their hearts are in the wrong place but because their faith is new.

When I was thirteen and got really involved with my new church, I had a group of friends my age who had just dedicated their lives to Christ. We were in the honeymoon stage. God meant everything to us all the time. We had no desires except for him. We wanted to do whatever he said. We were always happy. We were never discontent. We wanted to witness to everyone we came in contact with. We had faith that could move a mountain. We listened to Christian music all the time and shunned the "worldly" radio stations like Z100 or WPLJ (the popular music channels in the New York area back then).

We got together for birthday parties and other festive occasions and would spend hours praying with each other. I'm not trying to make fun of the experience—it was actually very nice—but there were times during our prayers when we would ask God for the silliest things. We begged to see angels. One time we were convinced that one of our friend's dogs was demon possessed, so we prayed to see the demons exorcised out of it. It was cute, I guess, and typical of thirteen-year-olds' immature religious thinking, but I know many people who grow up and have the same type of mentality. They don't want real spirituality, the kind that stretches their mind or their spirits or their capacity to believe or to do good. They ache for a type of mysticism that they are falsely convinced will make them believe in God.

Looking for Jesus in All the Wrong Places

Throughout time, humans have been infatuated with the inexplicable. Many spiritual movements have been based on what cannot be accounted for by sound reason. In 1981, a handful of children experienced apparitions in the small mountain village of Medjugorje, located in the former Yugoslavia. The story is that the Virgin Mary revealed herself to six children, the "visionaries," and told them ten specific "secrets" in addition to general messages about faith, prayer, fasting, and other cornerstone topics. These visions allegedly still continue, though there has been no scientific or any other type of evidence to establish their authenticity. By the early 1980s, Europe was familiar with this religious phantasm, and less than a decade later, word about this village's experience spread to the whole world. Millions of people have journeyed to this town to catch a glimpse of the Virgin Mary or the visionaries and to be touched by God in some miraculous way.

It's not for me to judge what's real and what's not. It's not for me to question the motives of the millions of people who flock to this village to find God or whatever it is they want to find. It's not for me to denounce the many people who say their lives were changed as a result of their pilgrimage. But the truth is, I get annoyed when people focus more on the unusual or supernatural instances of life or spirituality than on Jesus. I know he performed miracles and he healed people. But his message didn't revolve around the supernatural; it revolved around faith, love, peace, and compassion. It orbited around a meaningful spiritual conversion that called for living a life of abundance based on his message of faith, love, peace, and compassion.

But this gospel is not enough for us sometimes. It's sad to see the tantrums we throw in the absence of the spectacular. The sermon was okay, but we weren't moved to tears. The worship was fine, but no one was jumping, crying, laughing, dancing, shaking, or rolling in the Spirit. The prayer was all right, but no one moaned or groaned so loudly and powerfully that they could be heard across town.

Sometimes we expect Jesus to show up only in the sensational. So when weird things don't happen or we don't get incredibly emotional from a spiritual experience, we assume he never showed up. But in the midst of the common, the average, or the ordinary, Jesus did brush past us. He might have even tapped us on our shoulders. But in our reach for the drastic, we couldn't have recognized him, let alone have reached him.

And that's what happens sometimes when we are on the verge of believing in God or even in the middle of our faith journey. We don't want Jesus; we want other things. We want to run to a third world country where someone woke up one morning bearing stigmata. We want to go to the charismatic church where people are turning into human Jell-O and falling all over the building. We call 1-900 numbers and pray that the lady on TV with the skyscraper turban on her head will tell us if our spouse is cheating on us. We mail hundreds of dollars to heavily perspiring televangelists in return for "anointed" prayer cloths that will make our problems disappear.

I am not, in one way or another, judging or pointing an accusatory finger at a particular movement or doctrine. Let God be the final judge of these things. I just don't believe Jesus is sitting in the middle of them. I don't believe he grins from ear to ear when we are desperate to see a vision, or hear a prophecy, or pull out money from our pockets to guarantee us an answer for something. Why? Because it makes for a superficial faith, and when those things don't happen, we are apt to be annoyed by him, be angry with him, or even stop believing in him.

God is not just a wonder-worker. He is a savior. He is a deliverer. He is a comforter. He is merciful. If that isn't enough for you, you might as well shut the whole faith thing down and go back to wherever it is you came from. My friend,

51

miracles don't always occur. The supernatural doesn't always show up. This is a reality that many people don't want to admit, because, God forbid, Jesus and his message should be enough. It's boring. It's work. It lacks glitz and glamour. But remember what Jesus said: "Blessed are those who have not seen and yet have believed" (John 20:29 NIV). Blessed are those who keep plugging away in faith even though they don't get their miracle, their sign, their wonder, their quick fix, or their cure-all.

Sometimes You Just Gotta Be the Miracle

A lot of times my prayers are self-centered. I don't do this on purpose, but sometimes I am so overwhelmed by my problems that I don't know how to pray for other people without purging out my needs first. By the time I'm done surrendering all the big and small things that take up so much space in my mind and heart, I can end up too exhausted to pray for that person's job or this person's doctor's appointment or that person's relationship or this person's finances. This doesn't happen always, mind you, but lately it seems the norm. I don't like it one bit.

I'm reminded of something that happened to me about five years ago. One morning I was driving to my temp job at an employment agency. I wasn't too thrilled about the job, as I was paid pretty minimally and was stuck in an office for nine hours a day. I was assigned a particular project my supervisor described to me with so much passion and enthusiasm you'd have thought I was hired to find a cure for cancer. I was hired to use my expertise in office administration to file folders by last name instead of the way they were already being filed. My days consisted of carrying folders from one room in the building to another and organizing them in a metal file cabinet using my knowledge of what letters went where in the English alphabet. I was miserable, and I don't think anybody there liked me very much, but I was grateful for the cash.

As I was driving, I was begging God for a miracle. I needed one and I needed it fast. I had financial problems. My writing dream looked more like wishful thinking than something I could actually accomplish one day. My addiction was raging out of control. And I was back on antidepressants. But really, it was the financial mess that was freaking me out. So I prayed on my way to work. In the midst of my crying, my begging, my desperation, my whining, and my thinking that I was the only person in the world with such cataclysmic problems, I heard a voice deep down in my spirit say something that initially offended me.

"Be someone else's miracle."

Huh? And again. "Be someone else's miracle."

It was like telling a poor widow to give her next-door neighbor twenty bucks, or telling someone diagnosed with cancer to volunteer to read books to old people in nursing homes, or telling a person in their forties who never fell in love to help their twenty-two-year-old neighbor plan her engagement party. God has a pretty funny way of telling us to do things that seem to go against our nature or that don't make any sense. I think it's his way of being God in our lives. He gives us the opportunity to let him work in us so that we might be a blessing to someone else.

I don't mean to say that we should never think about ourselves, or always put everyone and everything ahead of our needs, or completely abandon our well-being and self-respect to help someone else. I'm just saying it might do us some good to forget about ourselves every now and then and think about what we can do for someone else. How can we be a miracle in the life of someone we may know or even a total stranger? What can we say to them that can encourage or remind them that not every human being is mean or selfish? What can we give them that might be the very thing they have been praying for? How can we serve them in ways that will meet a need they can't meet on their own?

Be someone else's miracle. It just might get you closer to getting yours, and not necessarily in the way you would ever expect.

3

The Terror of Trust

Those who believe that they believe in God, but without passion in their hearts, without anguish in mind, without uncertainty, without doubt, without an element of despair even in their consolation, believe in the God idea, not God himself.

Miguel de Unamuno

"Who is never going to let you go?" I ask four-year-old Kaitlyn as I wrap my wet arms around her in the deep end of the pool. "You are," she screeches at the top of her lungs. Then she immediately begs me to take her for a "ride" in the pool. I nuzzle her freckled nose with mine and stare into her turquoise blue eyes that stare back into mine with an expression of such delight you'd think Santa was coming. Kaitlyn can't swim and has been taught to stay away from the eight-feet-deep section of the pool that she refers to, with terrible fright, as the "drowning side." She is, however, allowed to be there with an adult, but Kaitlyn is very particular about who she lets accompany her. I'm one of the select few. It makes me feel quite cool.

A few months earlier, when I first met Kaitlyn, it took her a while to warm up to me, let alone to want me to accompany her in her parents' breathtaking pool. The first day we played together, my maternal instincts kicked in, and I wouldn't let her stray more than a few inches from me. Then we started playing a game I called "Who is never going to let you go?" That, of course, was me. She caught on quickly and began to trust me. I'd throw her up in the air. I'd swish her around the pool by her cute little feet. I'd swim in the deep end with her on my back, her fingernails digging straight into the flesh of my neck. Every few minutes, she would look up at me with her rapturous eyes and ask, "Who's never going to let me go?" And I would reply with total confidence, "I am, Kaitlyn, I am. I am never going to let you go."

Something happens as we get older. Life. It takes us for a wild spin down winding roads, through blistering deserts, up rugged mountains, down dark valleys, and of course through seasons of bliss and paradise. But the tough times are probably simultaneously the most frustrating and life-changing. We all experience something that challenges our spirits to easily believe in the goodness of life or the goodness of God or even in his existence. Divorce. Death. Rape. Cancer. Bankruptcy. Betrayal. Through these experiences life whips out a tool from its pocket and starts chipping away at, among so many things, our innocence, our security, and especially our faith. And as jagged piece after jagged piece falls to the wayside, something more happens than simply life showing up.

We fear. We stop trusting. We become defensive. We question motives. We do whatever we have to do to protect ourselves, our emotions, our sanity, and our future. The protective shell we all have to guard our hearts—which is really not completely a terrible thing—hardens like the shell of a tortoise, and we start losing joy, peace, and faith. We misplace our wonder on purpose. We toss aside our belief, far away from our immediate reach. These things pose too much of a risk for us to keep around, and so we chuck them out in the trash in order to never hurt like that again.

It's easy for a four-year-old to wrap her tiny arms around my neck and trust me with making sure she doesn't drown in the deep end. She knows I won't let her go. She knows I won't stop paying attention. She knows I love her too much not to protect her. When we are born, we really have nothing to rely on to survive in this world other than our parents or our caretakers. Trusting others is innate. We don't even think about it. It's when we get older and experience life that the inborn deposit of trust is withdrawn little by little.

Take a thirty-year-old who just got out of a messy divorce because her husband was cheating on her while she was caring for five kids under the age of seven. Chances are, unfortunately, that she probably is going to have a tough time trusting the next man in her life—if she even wants one. Take a forty-year-old who was given a bad deal and was let go from the company he dedicated twenty years to. His trust in the goodness of people or in upper management to do the right thing is probably going to be at least somewhat flushed down the toilet. Ages are not the point, of course. It doesn't matter how old you are. Anyone sucker-punched by a crummy life event is affected by it to some extent. And it's usually in the area of trust.

Now add spirituality to the mix. As people of faith, we are taught to trust in God . . . no matter what. And the God we are supposed to trust in is a deity we cannot see, hear, or feel. He is virtually invisible. We are taught to trust in him that our prayers will get answered, that life will ultimately be good, and that our needs will be met. A hymn was written in the late 1800s about how sweet it is to trust in Jesus:

> 'Tis so sweet to trust in Jesus,
> Just to take Him at His word;
> Just to rest upon His promise;
> And to know, "Thus saith the Lord."
>
> Jesus, Jesus, how I trust Him!
> How I've proved Him o'er and o'er!
> Jesus, Jesus, precious Jesus!
> O for grace to trust Him more![1]

But is trusting in the unknown really that sweet? Is it as easy as it seems? Is it something that should come naturally, without hesitation, and with full confidence? Is it as simple as closing your eyes, uttering a prayer for help, and holding out your arms in faith that someone is going to catch you or never let you go? Does the act of trusting in God come without an element of fear? And if you say with your mouth that you trust in God but still feel an overwhelming knot in the pit of your stomach, are you really putting out sincere faith? Is that the true measure of trust?

While some people have an easier time trusting in God than others, the reality is that it can be a scary process. Especially when you are catapulted into a messy or painful life experience without a smidgen of understanding and without the slightest glimpse of what lies ahead. Especially when God seems hidden, if you even believe he is there at all. Especially if situations are beyond your power and control to fix. I don't mean to sound like "Debbie Downer," but sometimes trusting in God isn't really all that sweet. Sometimes it can be so scary it just might seem easier to put our trust in anything other than him.

Why Bother Trusting in God at All?

I had a conversation with a good friend of mine the other day. We were talking about making the commitment to spend time in prayer and meditation on a consistent basis, preferably every day. She said something that shocked me but that I appreciated because it was so honest. Here was a woman who was beautiful and very intelligent, was self-made, had an amazing family, and had lots of self-confidence. She was raised to be a go-getter, and as a wife, a mother, and a career woman, she was just that. She hustled and she bustled. She was basically a real-life Wonder Woman.

"Sometimes I don't think I need God," she told me. She believed in God. There was no doubt about that. She just happened to be very capable on her own. Tears dripped down her cheeks almost in slow motion as she continued. "I just think I can do everything on my own. I mean, I really have no choice. I have to be good at everything. But deep down inside I know that's not true. I know I need God. So why don't I act like it?"

There was nothing wrong with her self-belief. As a matter of fact, I admire this woman plenty, because I wish I had as much confidence in myself as she does in herself.

But we have a tendency, when we start relying completely on ourselves, to believe we don't need God. Why do we need to trust in someone we can't see or hear? Why trust in someone who doesn't respond to our every beck and call? Why deal with the raging emotions of fear and tumult in praying to a God we sometimes only hope will listen? Why settle for wishful thinking when we can do fine on our own . . . when we can weather the toughest of storms because we are tough enough . . . when we can micromanage life's stresses because we are organized enough . . . when we can deal with heartache, pain, and loss because we are emotional giants? Who needs God when we have ourselves and can provide our own escape hatches, plans B–Z, and emergency exits?

We all carry some sense of self-sufficiency. In this dog-eat-dog world where we have to be the best, where we have to execute, and where we have to be on top of our game, we do need to be competent, efficient, independent, and strong. These are good things. I know that God doesn't want his children to be a bunch of lazy, insecure people who do nothing except twiddle their thumbs and complain about how ugly, dumb, or slow they are. I just think we miss the boat as it concerns spirituality when we start to believe we are invincible and we don't need the hand of Providence. It reminds me of the verse in the Bible that says, "Some trust in chariots and some in horses, but we trust in the name of the LORD our God" (Ps. 20:7 NIV). Some trust in their looks. Some trust in their talent. Some trust even in their positive attitude. You can call me insecure and you can say that my faith is a crutch, but there is only one thing I root my core faith in, and that is God.

We all have rugs in our lives that will be pulled out from under us at some point. We are all hanging on ropes of which we will one day feel the end. We will all endure some circumstance that is going to leave us saying, "I don't know what to do. I don't know where to go. I have no power to change, to fix, or to make this particular situation disappear. I need help—God's help." Rest assured, no one is immune from experiencing these sucker-punch moments. And if we need God in those turbulent moments, why don't we think we still need him when life is relatively carefree?

I'm reminded of Jean Dominique-Bauby, the man on whose life the movie *The Diving Bell and the Butterfly* is based. A hotshot editor of the French fashion magazine *Elle*, he suffered a massive stroke at the age of forty-three. It left him mute and paralyzed by way of a disease called "Locked-in Syndrome." While his brain fully functioned, he was rendered immobile and practically powerless to communicate. Jean could only see out of and blink his left eye. This is how he eventually learned to share his thoughts. Someone would recite the French alphabet to him, and he would blink his eye when he heard the letters of the words he wanted to say. He used that method to write his memoir, which was published only two days before he died.

Jean had it all. His career was skyrocketing. He had a beautiful family. He had a wide variety of gorgeous lovers. He drove fancy cars. He was constantly flocked by models, celebrities, and rock stars. He was a cool guy, and everyone who was anyone wanted to hang around him. Then, in literally a few seconds, he lost everything and was forced to spend the rest of his life lying on a hospital bed, unable to move and unable to speak. All Jean was able to do was think, and he was sometimes haunted, sometimes soothed by his imagination and his past.

In one part of the movie, he said, "Today, my life feels like a string of near-misses. Women I was unable to love, opportunities I failed to seize, moments of happiness I let drift away. A race whose result I knew beforehand, but failed to pick the winner. Had I been blind and deaf, or did the harsh light of disaster make me find my true nature?" It's a powerful statement, but perhaps not for the reason you're thinking. I'm not mentioning this to talk about the moral dilemmas of this guy's life or to stress the importance of living life to the fullest, doing the right thing, or keeping your priorities straight.

What I took away from his story was that stuff happens—pretty scary, unfair, and even evil stuff. And when that happens, I don't care how smart, stunning, charming, rich, educated, or tough we are; the situation is out of our control and there is nothing in us that can repair it. This is why we need a core of belief. This is why faith is so important, why trusting in God—even one who may feel, at times, as real as a fable—is important. We need to understand that we do not control this thing called life. We won't always have the answers. We won't always have the wherewithal to kiss our boo-boos and make it all better.

Sometimes we don't trust in God because of a deeper reason than our self-sufficiency. Sometimes we've been hurt. We are disappointed with God because he didn't show up that one time that rocked our world. The particular prayer didn't get answered. Our friend ended up dying of cancer. We couldn't get out of bankruptcy and had to watch the bank foreclose on our home. Maybe we are wounded because God is silent and we feel like he is off snorkeling somewhere in the Bahamas.

And sometimes we don't trust in God because we simply don't know how. It doesn't feel as easy or as simple as perhaps we are taught it should. Maybe our trusting God looks like begging or whining. Maybe it looks something like half wondering and half trusting. Or half feeling peaceful and half feeling worried.

What Trust Can Look Like

I think about the time I spent as an incognito churchgoer at a faith-hyped church. Although it had satisfied my emotionally starving soul because of the pomp and circumstance of the services, it didn't help with my frustration in experiencing the silence of God. I had not gone to church in a few years and started attending this one in particular because of the reports I'd heard. People left services feeling strengthened, empowered, and on fire. I figured it'd be a good start for me to help shift my exasperation at God to something else, something better.

But I felt like a loser in the church. Everybody who sat in the pews seemed to have it all together. They seemed to know all the faith "rules." It seemed they knew exactly how to be effective in their faith affirmations so they got whatever it was they needed or wanted. These people stood tall with squared shoulders and chins pointed upward. There were no telltale signs of a struggling saint present within the congregation—except, of course, for me.

Now I just knew there were people in there who were camouflaging their weakness, because every now and then the pastor would douse his sermon with admonishments to "Just have faith," "Stop being a wimp and believe in God," "You have to stop worrying and start believing," "Enough crying, whining, and complaining; just trust God." It sounded great in theory, but how do you wake up after a night of tossing and turning and just have faith? How do you spontaneously have an "aha" moment in the middle of the day and start trusting God with as minimal effort as trusting that your local mail carrier is going to bring you your mail?

Clearly, I was doing something wrong. There was something I couldn't quite get, and it scared me. I was going through a variety of personal problems, on the verge of making really important decisions that would ultimately change the course of my life, and so depressed it was a chore just to drag myself out of bed in the morning. My prayers were blubbering messes. I needed help, and I knew what I was supposed to do. I knew I had to trust God, but while I was trying to have faith that he would somehow intervene in my circumstances, I didn't feel peace. I felt anxious. Nervous. Tired. And frightened. My stomach was in knots before, after, and during prayers. Trust God? You've got to be kidding me. Why trust in something or someone that clearly wasn't around?

When I was at church, I heard people all around me singing, "Victory is mine, victory is mine, victory today is mine," with shiny smiles and in perfect harmony. All I could manage to whisper was a muffled, "Rock of ages, cleft for me, let me hide myself in Thee." Now, I knew there was some weight in my faith. Since I didn't give up on God completely, and I didn't stop "trying" to trust (though I believe my efforts were failing miserably), there had to be some level of belief in my psyche.

I was in a desperate position. I needed to trust in God, but he wasn't saying or doing anything to ease the fears I was going through with this whole faith thing. I figured if I mimicked whatever the people around me were doing or saying, perhaps I could gain some spiritual muscle. So I faked it until (hopefully soon) I would make it. I clapped my hands. I jumped up and down. I nodded at the punchy and witty comments the pastor made. If I was feeling especially bold, I even shouted out an amen or two. I would repeat prayers of strength and confidence, casting out my fears "in the name of Jesus." Every Sunday afternoon I left the church ready to conquer the world, but the evenings would come, and as soon as I realized nothing was changing in my circumstances and God still seemed absent, I'd cower in shame and limp away from my superficial confidence like a wounded animal.

So began the premature struggle of my faith and trust in a God I couldn't quite figure out and definitely couldn't see or hear. But there was something more important than the wrestling match I was having with trying to trust in him and achieving some level of security that he was listening and would work in me. I needed to understand that the fear I had was normal. Nothing was wrong with me. I wasn't a terrible Christian because of it. And God certainly didn't throw his hands up in the air and roll his eyes at my anxiety, saying, "Good grief, woman. Can't you get it already? What's wrong with you?" Granted, he didn't say much of anything, but I did learn he wasn't a God who could be driven to the brink of insanity just hearing or watching folks who felt normal human emotions.

And you know what? Eventually the anxiety subsided after I realized that some measure of fear in trusting God was okay. I also came to the understanding that sometimes trusting in God looks different from person to person. Sure, maybe Lisa has the easiest time believing God for particular things or even that he is real and active in our lives, but Bob isn't any less faith-oriented because every once in a while he gets upset or worried or wonders if God truly hears him. Don't get me wrong. I'm not advocating being in a constant state of worry or depression in your spirituality. I'm just talking about our reactions to life circumstances that have the power to overwhelm or even crush our spirits. If you are going through a particularly traumatic event, the picture of trusting God might not look so pretty or perfect. Let it be what it is. Just don't stop believing.

Years ago, I connected with a wonderful couple named Matt and Debbie. They had been married for like a million years, and both had incredibly outgoing and comedic personalities. There was something really special about them, and both emanated a refreshing and comforting inner peace. When I met this couple, I was quick to learn their story. We all have a story, but some are more heartbreaking than others. Their story went beyond heartbreaking, and it caused me to question what made them such positive people of faith.

Debbie gave birth to triplets. All were diagnosed with cystic fibrosis, a chronic disease that affects the lungs and digestive system. A defective gene causes the body to produce unusually thick, sticky mucus that ultimately leads to life-threatening lung infections. It's a loud and obnoxious sickness. People afflicted by it cough nonstop, often producing large globs of phlegm. Breathing is difficult and painful because of the progressive disability of the lungs. People who have this illness can be expected to live only until their midthirties, if they're lucky.

One of Matt and Debbie's sons died when he was eighteen years old. The second son died at twenty. When I met this couple, these two sons had already passed away and the third son was struggling through his own long and hard fight with the disease. I saw the son on occasion. He looked like he was wasting away, but he had the same twinkle in his eye and witty sense of humor that his parents had. He relied on a portable oxygen tank to breathe but never wanted any pity or help from anyone else if he could do whatever he needed to do for himself.

For the last part of his life, he was a patient at Duke University Hospital awaiting a lung and heart transplant. I frequently spoke to Matt and Debbie during that time. They couldn't eat. They couldn't sleep. Debbie refused to leave the hospital because her other two sons had died there. Matt wanted to be there as much as he could, but he had a full-time job. It's not easy to work in a blue-collar field and compete with stacking medical bills, uncooperative insurance companies, and government health care. So what did they do? They prayed, they trusted God, and they waited, not knowing how quickly death was going to appear this time around. And in the meantime, life continued its boisterous roar and speedy motion, paying no mind to their circumstances. Mail needed to be opened. Phone calls needed to be returned. Work meetings had to be attended. Grocery shopping had to be done. They battled against death, disease, and the daily routine of life that cannot be ignored. Whenever Matt and I spoke about his faith, he always told me more or less the same thing. While he believed in God and his goodness . . . while he believed in miracles . . . while he believed in the power of prayer . . . and while he trusted God to do something . . . he always qualified these statements by saying, "Sometimes I just want to ask the man upstairs what he thinks he's doing . . . and that's exactly what I'm going to do when my time comes." He referred to God as "the man upstairs" with such sincerity, passion, angst, anger, and a strange but very real form of trust.

There was no sugarcoating of their son's situation. Matt and Debbie were waiting for a life to end so their boy would get a shot at living just a little while longer. One person had to die so another could live. And there they were, trusting the man upstairs even though two graves had been dug and a plot of land was ready for the third grave. The situation left me speechless and humbled. I never knew exactly what to say to this wonderful couple, but I always admired their faith. They didn't shout it out or raise their voices saying "Hallelujah" every two seconds. They didn't throw out annoying Christian cliches. They didn't deny their pain and frustration. But they did have a solid and sure belief that gently stirred at the bottoms of their spirits. Maybe it doesn't seem that solid to you, but in the deepest part of my heart, I believed it was good enough.

How exactly are you supposed to trust in God while feelings of anxiety swarm around your head and heart like a swarm of bees knocked out of their nest with brute force? How do you swat away the thoughts that seem to possess your mind? Thoughts like: *It's not going to work out. You'll see, you'll be devastated. You'd better give up now; don't think it's going to get better.* How? You simply try (usually it's a long period of "trying") and trust God that he'll do the rest (whatever that "rest" is, exactly). Sometimes trying means repeating Bible verses in your head until the words run into each other like a train wreck. Other times it means occupying your brain with thoughts other than the ones that have cluttered it and made thinking with clarity almost impossible. Maybe it means thinking of or praying for other people who have asked for your prayers or who need them. Sometimes it takes learning or remembering to breathe.

No magic formula or algebraic solution exists to make the trusting as easy as possible. You try, pray, believe, and wait (in no particular order). Keep believing in the impossible. Keep believing that God still has you nestled in his hands. Keep believing that the day, the hour, the second will come when your fears start to hush, because eventually they do simmer down. Eventually your spirit will get more quiet and peaceful than frightened and desperate. Just give yourself a little break when the getting to that "eventually" part really stinks.

Sometimes It's Very Sweet

I wonder who suggested heading to the beach that day. Was it Louisa or her husband? Perhaps their four-year-old daughter, Lily, had tugged her mama's dress hard enough, stamped her feet loud enough, and offered an irresistible puppy dog look that had convinced her parents to take that fatal trip. Regardless of the whys, they went. More than likely it was an absolutely ordinary day, probably a perfect day to soak in a few rays, take a cool dip by the water's edge, maybe play some catch. Yet out of that ordinary day, a hero emerged.

A hero who intended to sacrifice his own life for the sake of another. Was it a noble gesture? Absolutely. Did it all work out to everyone's benefit? No.

The three of them were eating a picnic lunch, probably exchanging giggles, smiles, hugs, and kisses. The father may have been commenting on how delicious the sandwiches were that his two favorite girls had made. Little Lily may have been asking when she'd be allowed in the water. There may have been silent offerings of thanksgiving for the blessing of having such a wonderful family.

One shrill cry shattered the entire peaceful scene: "Help!" This sweet family saw a boy violently thrashing about in the water. He was drowning. The father of this family, overcome with a heroic instinct, ran to the water, dived in, and swam out to save the little boy's life. The rescue never happened. Because of the boy's uncontrollable hysteria, he pulled the man who tried to save his life under the water, and together they drowned. The yelling and thrashing and hysteria caused a terror-stricken crowd to gather by the shoreline. No one was more petrified, however, than Louisa and her daughter, Lily. They watched the man they loved more than their own lives fighting for his life. With a last gasp of breath, he plunged deep beneath the water's surface.

Louisa was left a widow and a single parent to little Lily. Louisa couldn't support them on her own. The day came when their financial resources ran completely dry and they didn't have a single thing to eat. I'm reminded of a widow in the Bible, living during a season of drought in the nation of Israel. This was a woman whom God had not forgotten about, although to the widow that didn't feel nor seem to be the case. This woman was in her home, preparing her last meal for herself and her son, when the prophet Elijah walked in the front door. He was hungry and asked for something to eat. It seemed quite brash, and the widow explained her situation to him. She didn't have any extra food for him. Then Elijah piped up in another audacious move and told her that if she gave that last meal to him, she wouldn't run out of food. We don't know if she looked at him as if he were crazy or if she was so full of despair that she figured, why not? But she gave in and trusted what was ultimately God's Word. If you read the story in 1 Kings 17, you'll find out the widow wasn't disappointed.

Fast-forward hundreds of centuries, and Louisa Stead seemed to be mirroring that situation. I'm sure she must have bit her lip and forced her tears to run dry when the reality of the situation sank in. Her husband was dead. She had no money. There was no food left. Where was God and why wasn't he providing? Perhaps more importantly, why did he let death have its way without intervening?

That same day, when she opened her front door, Louisa found a thick envelope full of cash and a basketful of food on her doorstep. God had not disappointed. He had made provisions for her. He had heard her heart cries.

Do you honestly think for one minute that Louisa's immediate reaction to watching her husband die or her initial feelings in the midst of her ensuing hardships came without a pinch of resentment or doubt? Do you think she effortlessly raised her hands in sweet surrender and graciously accepted such life happenstance without the initial raise of a fist and the repetitive booming questions of why? Unless you have a master's degree in naiveté and ignorance, you must agree when I say, of course not.

I'm sure Louisa ran through the whole gamut of emotions— from shock to grief to anger—and directed many of them toward God. Who wouldn't have done that? But after a time, as should be the case in our own particular circumstances, the anger and the unrelenting questions and even the spite must be toned down, and the time comes to surrender our defensive weapons of fear and learn to trust in God.

While Louisa's tears would still need to be wiped dry and uncertainty lay ahead, she knew she'd be better off to trust in Jesus. With that, she started to write one of my favorite hymns, "'Tis So Sweet to Trust in Jesus."

> I'm so glad I learned to trust Thee,
> Precious Jesus, Savior, Friend;
> And I know that Thou art with me,
> Wilt be with me to the end.
>
> Jesus, Jesus how I trust Him!
> How I've proved Him over and o'er!
> Jesus, Jesus, precious Jesus!
> O for grace to trust Him more![2]

Things will turn out the way they are supposed to whether influenced by our faith, life, or God. So why is trusting in God so important? Because it's a release of our will. It's an uplifting of our hands in surrender. It's a measure, however slight, of our faith in the God we can't hear or see. And that is what God honors. Do we have proof or a guarantee that our trust in him will result in the perfect plan? No. How can we—as human beings experiencing human emotions, feelings, sentiments, and thoughts—know this for sure? We can't. But we believe nonetheless, and that is the type of faith God honors. The trust that we've placed in the invisible should not be placed because we've been taught it should. The true measure of trust is when we're at our last sigh, when we're left without assurances, when we've realized that blind trust is all we have, and we move forward in it, taking one small step at a time.

Trusting in God is both scary and sweet. But you usually can never really experience the sweet part if you don't experience the scary part. God is in control, and we do need him. Believing those two statements is what ultimately transforms our initial trepidation into a sense of peace. Our shaky faith can be mysteriously strengthened in the absence of what we believe would solidify it and in the presence of a hope in God. However scared or nervous trusting in an invisible God makes you feel, just keep believing in spite of all that. Without a doubt, doing so means you are headed in the right direction.

4

Faith: Where Is My Money-Back Guarantee?

Faith is not a guarantee that our questions will be answered. It's a relatively blind belief in what is unseen, unheard, and unspoken. The guarantee is that our verbiage is not received by deaf ears. Perhaps that's not the peachiest answer, but the reality.

I once asked a group of people from a wide variety of life experiences and religious backgrounds what they have faith in and why. I found the answers to be quite fascinating:

"Earth. I believe that the spinning ball of life on which we exist will thrive well beyond the history of humankind and whatever other species are to come."

"I have faith in a just and orderly and good universe—although often I can't see the justness and orderliness and goodness at first glance."

"I have faith in the Lord because I don't know what I would believe in if not him. Who he says he is, who the Word says he is, how I have experienced him in my own life. He has rescued me and set me free. He has drawn my boundaries and expanded them."

"I have faith in humanity—in our basic needs and desires. I believe in the full range of humanity, from the best and the goodness that humanity can deliver, to the evil and destruction that can also be delivered. I have faith in a higher level of consciousness, be it God or a Higher Power, but a power that is grander and far superior to humanity. I believe in all of this because the more I try to understand our humanistic nature and our spiritual nature, the less I understand."

"Faith is an abstract, a tertiary sum of hope and love. There are plenty of things people have put faith in, whether it's a God, their career, their family, their spouses. For me, I don't place faith in the intangible. Thus, God, religion, and the like fall to the wayside for me. Instead, I place faith in things I can control, like myself, and stable things like my family."

"I have faith that good things happen to good people, and that it carries over in the end . . . meaning if there is a judgment day that we will be viewed by our actions as opposed to our faiths or beliefs. It seems to be a much more reasonable contingency for numerous reasons."

"Religiously, I'm struggling right now to say the church because of past conversations and experiences with others over the past couple years. I have faith in a lot of things, but it comes down to faith in people. Not just anybody, but faith

74

in good people. I really have faith that in the end this creates a better place and will help outlast lots of other 'bad.'"

"I believe in friendship and in few but unique friends. Why? Because I guess that your friends are the family you choose, the ones whom you are connected to without any type of further interest but only the desire to share good and bad with."

"Right off the bat I thought, 'Of course, Jesus,' but I have to admit I have faith in myself and, to be quite selfish, my looks. As insecure and stupid as it sounds, I guess I have faith that the way I look will take me places or give me some confidence in myself. I've always thought that I am strong enough to get by on my own, if things fail or fall around me; I know I have faith in myself to pull it all together."

"I have faith in love. I have to. Yes, there are so many examples of failed love, twisted romance, misguided affection. But if I were to dwell on those there would be nothing to believe in. Love exists; I believe it. I have faith in second chances. If I didn't have faith in this, I'd be doomed."

"Nothing. I don't have faith in anything."

Think about the questions yourself. What do you have faith in and why? Who or what do you trust in?

Why Is Faith in God So Important?

Some have faith in God. Others have faith in friends or good times or science. What I want to focus on is faith in God—the good part of faith and the not-so-good part of faith. That Christians would use faith as a proverbial Band-Aid—as some sort of medicinal relief that would act as the catalyst for the surety of answered prayers, the eternal elimination of doubts, and the answering of unanswerable questions—is nothing short of hogwash. What is faith? The dictionary calls it "belief that does not rest on logical proof or material evidence." The book of Hebrews calls it "the substance of things *hoped* for, the evidence of things *not seen*" (Heb. 11:1 KJV, emphasis added). I like placing the emphasis on the "hoped for" and "not seen" parts.

Faith doesn't seem picture perfect, though we would all probably feel a little more comfortable on our journey if it was. In fact, faith might even seem a little flimsy at certain times. One thing is for sure: it definitely is not as formulaic as most people probably think it should be. As a matter of fact, the crux of Christianity rests on redemption through faith, through believing, instead of having it all together or adopting and religiously abiding by a set of rules and regulations.

I've seen many people abuse the word *faith* by defining it as a confidence that all things should work out without a share of challenges, or as an immediate relief from doubt, or as something that is only effective when in action 100 percent of the time with 100 percent solidity. I like what Frederick Buechner wrote: "Whether your faith is that there is a God or that there is not a God, if you don't have any doubts you are either kidding yourself or asleep. Doubts are the ants in the pants of faith. They keep it awake and moving."

Faith isn't a concrete block of surety. It's not a blueprint you can whip out whenever you need to perfectly navigate through life. It definitely doesn't come with a road map. And guess what? It doesn't have a guarantee. On the surface, this can seem like a disheartening statement, but it's a reality. The truth, however, is that it's not as depressing as it seems. Sure, spirituality without the need for faith just might be an easier path to walk on. I mean, really, who wants to believe in the unknown without a promissory note? Who wants to keep holding on to belief without seeing the answers in the back of the textbook?

In the course of our daily lives, we take conscious and sub-conscious leaps of faith. Does it mean that a grand gesture of our faith will result with us getting what we want? Does having faith mean life will always be great and good will always pre-vail over evil? Does it mean that our dreams, our prayers, our visions, our needs, or our wants will always come to fruition? No. Faith does not come with a money-back guarantee. Life, for that matter, has no guarantees. Whether you believe in God or don't believe in God, you understand that stuff happens beyond your control and nothing can guarantee a certain outcome.

Is Faith That Important?

So why have faith? What's the point? If no guarantee is at-tached to the activity of believing, and it can take so much effort and energy to do it, does having faith even matter? And why is faith in something so important to most people, as many studies have shown?

Over decades of research at Harvard Medical School and other universities, experts have determined a definite rela-tionship between faith and good health. Dr. Herbert Benson, president of the Mind/Body Institute at Beth Israel Deaconess Medical Center in Boston, says, "Between 50 to 90 percent of all diseases can be affected by patient belief, and 90 percent of Americans report that their strongest belief is in God." At a three-day conference called "Spirituality and Healing in Medicine," sponsored by Harvard Medical School and the Mind/Body Medical Institute, leading researchers, psy-chologists, physicians, clergy, and educators involved in this topic concluded that "faith and the human spirit cannot be separated from clinical care and medicine."[1]

Faith has also been linked to a longer life. Dr. Harold G. Koenig, founding director of the Center for the Study of Religion, Spirituality and Health at Duke University Medical Center, offered, "At least six studies in the past two years have found a relationship between involvement in a religious community and longer survival. Religious beliefs and activities are associated with better mental and physical health in the vast majority of the studies."[2]

Countless studies suggest that most Americans find faith very important to them. It is apparently so integrated into every aspect of our lives that it is influencing political views and how people vote. Additionally, faith is such a big deal that in February of 2008, researchers at the University of Oxford began the development of a major new study investigating why people believe in God using a scientific approach. This team was given a grant of $3.7 million to fund the project.

Faith in God is obviously important to laypeople and to the brains behind the informative studies and mounds of research regarding this topic. Faith is both comforting and mysterious, and it is not something to be taken lightly. There is a difference between simple faith and naive faith. Simple faith means having our core values grounded in God without denying the reality that having faith can be a challenge. Naive faith is thinking that if we do X, Y, and Z, our faith will guarantee us whatever we feel we need guaranteed.

Naive faith is similar to believing that if you use certain dating strategies, you will find "the one," the feelings will be reciprocated, and you will walk down the aisle toward a happily-ever-after paradise. Single people, for example, are repeatedly encouraged to "play the game." Playing this so-called game—which is nothing more than hopeful manipulation—will not necessarily result in getting the man or woman of our dreams. Just because we wait three days to call, or act real busy or important on purpose, or never let them see us without makeup or in sweaty gym clothes does not mean we will automatically receive the affection of our crush or love interest. Can these strategies help create romance or spark interest? Certainly. But more importantly, sometimes they don't.

I'm sure all of you single people understand where I'm coming from. I'm sure you have experienced times when you've religiously followed the dating rules, said the right things, acted the best way possible, and looked beautiful all the time, but still you did not land the person of your dreams. You didn't get the third date. You didn't get a return phone call. The sweet words once whispered in your ear fell silent. The interest in you disappeared. Why? What did you do wrong? Did you not deserve that person, date, or phone call? Did you possibly neglect a particular dating "regulation," and so you now spend your Saturday nights watching *Law & Order* reruns?

This idea can apply to our faith walk, specifically as it concerns God. He is mysterious, powerful, and beyond our total understanding. We sometimes cannot comprehend why he does what he does or why he doesn't do what we think he should. Even if we read all the spiritual books out there that offer us a step-by-step plan for how to get our prayers answered, how to find out what his will is, or how to overcome a particular challenge, that doesn't always mean that life will turn out the way we think it should. The one guarantee we do have is his presence.

Unanswered Prayers Do Not Necessarily Equal Lack of Faith

"You didn't get your answer because of your lack of faith." When I worked in the legal department of a corporation in the early 2000s, a prayer chain was communicated via internal email. Each day I read the twenty or so requests that came in.

Someone's husband died. A teenager lost a leg in a serious car wreck. A baby was born with Down syndrome. A couple was struggling with divorce. This person was diagnosed with cancer. That person would be undergoing a triple bypass surgery on Wednesday. It was quite dismal to read through the list and see all the bad things that were happening to relatively good people. But it was also nice knowing there was a spiritual community out there who cared enough to make a commitment to pray for these people.

What used to really irk me were the whispers I heard in the halls or bullish reply emails that were sent back regarding the prayer requests. I'd like to think that these folks had good intentions and weren't completely consumed with ignorance or even stupidity, but who knows? In response to the person offering up the prayer requests, however grand or small the needs were, a handful of people would say things like, "Well, have you prayed for healing?" "Do you really have enough faith in God for the miracle you're asking for?" "Is there some sin in your life that may be causing this problem or preventing God from stepping in?" "Is there any part of you that doubts that God can take care of your situation?" What was going on? These people were trying to justify a terrible happening with an absence of faith or a not-quite-good-enough faith. To me, these questions were so ridiculous they made me want to scream.

My tolerance level for people who are ignorant, especially relating to spiritual matters and the mystery of it all, is quite low. Every time I heard these horrible questions others asked, I wanted to smack the stupid out of the ones who were asking them. We may have sharp gut instincts and a high level of discernment, but when a friend, colleague, or stranger is going through something highly traumatic, what right do we have to judge the measure or sincerity of their faith? How on earth can we tell them they are doing something wrong because things aren't working out? Are we that wise? Are we that intuitive? Are we that knowledgeable? I'm not talking about those people who really know the person who is asking for prayer and are really responding in wisdom and with the right intentions. I'm talking about the people—you know who they are—who are so quick to accuse others of spiritual mistakes, wayward turns, or not experiencing a faith that mimics their own (because clearly, these ignorant people are sure they know exactly what faith means, looks like, and how it is supposed to be acted out).

Think about it. A baby is still in the intensive care unit covered with a mass of intertwining tubes and IVs like a medicinal spider web—does that mean the inconsolable mother didn't pray or had no faith or stole some Post-it notes from the office? Was it because a man did not pray hard enough that his wife died of leukemia three months after they got married? Did you forget to disinfect your life by spraying redemptive Lysol over each and every single one of your sins, and so you are forced to deal with a divorce instead of a reconcilable marriage? Or do things just go wrong sometimes? Or does life just happen? Or do we, most times, not have life quite figured out and need to take it one day at a time?

Romans 12:3 tells us that God gives every human being a certain measure of faith. What that measure is exactly, we don't know. I can't tell you how big or small your measure is, and guess what? You can't tell me what my measure looks like. Most often, though, people's capacity for faith looks more like a Dixie cup than the cargo bed of a monster pickup truck. This doesn't mean that we are people who are naturally disinclined to engage in faith. It just means that sometimes belief can be hard to execute. Sometimes our faith can be shadowed by flecks of doubt. Sometimes believing in or for something is more challenging for us than for our next-door neighbor. This, unfortunately, can cause us to question whether we really believe.

The book of Mark records a conversation exchanged between Jesus and a man who had a son with epilepsy. Some translations say the boy was demon-possessed, but most historians conclude the boy was suffering from a severe form of epilepsy. At one point, this distraught father approaches Jesus in the middle of an arguing and bickering crowd. Jesus seems more peeved than anything, as a cacophony of voices clamor for attention to get their point across. Jesus turns to the man and asks him what all the fuss is about.

The father, holding the hand of his wide-eyed son, tells Jesus that his son is suffering from demonic possession. He has frequent seizures, he foams at the mouth, and the poor child's body becomes as stiff as a board after he is violently shaken by the seizures. The father looks Jesus straight in the eye and tells him, "So I went to your disciples and asked them to do something, but nothing happened. Their prayers didn't work, and my son is in the same condition" (see Mark 9:18). The man is completely desperate at this point and begs Jesus to do something.

Jesus mutters in exasperation, "You faithless people! How long must I be with you? How long must I put up with you?" (Mark 9:19). He is referring to the murmuring crowd and to his disciples. After these men had tried unsuccessfully to work their magic and use whatever power they had to heal this boy, they shrugged their shoulders, probably kicked the dirt with their sandals in frustration or embarrassment, and sent the man away. The poor father. His faith had probably been practically depleted at that point. Practically? Sure. Completely? No.

The man doesn't turn away and go back where he came from. He doesn't curse the disciples and call them a bunch of dummies, hypocrites, or fakes. He doesn't go to the local witch doctor, or anywhere else for that matter. More importantly, he doesn't give up. The man charges forward and meets with the head honcho, the big cheese, the ultimate source. If anybody could do anything, it would have to be Jesus. But while he is relaying his story, for probably the umpteenth time, his faith is dueling internal struggles. It's the battle between faith and doubt. Doubt and faith. Emily Dickinson put it this way: "We both believe and disbelieve a hundred times an hour, which keeps faith nimble."[3]

This man's faith is nimble enough that he is able to abruptly turn his heels around and away from the stammering disciples and bolt in Jesus's direction to beg him for help. Jesus tells the father to bring his son over to him. After hearing the man's story, Jesus says something like, "Well, of course I can help your situation, but the true question is whether you believe I can." In others words, "All things are possible, young man—do you dare believe? Do you dare take a chance on the impossible? Do you dare have faith in the laughing and scheming face of the unknown?" And the man replies in what I believe is one of the most poignant statements defining the essence of truth faith: "I do believe, but help me overcome my unbelief!" (Mark 9:24).

Jesus didn't initiate the conversation by reminding this man of the many miracles he had pulled off. He didn't justify his authority as the Son of Man and the Son of God. He didn't question the man's faith as part of the problem in the inability of the disciples to heal his ailing son. Jesus told him that faith is the crux of dealing with problematic situations. And then he challenged him to the duel. Faith versus doubt. Doubt versus faith. The man gave Jesus all he could give—the measure of faith he was given and the percentage of doubt that trailed behind it. Jesus recognized both, understood both, and came to his aid.

"You don't have enough faith." To the ones who throw that ignorant statement out there, know that some doubt is intertwined with believing. The beauty is that Christ is the one who, with nothing less than compassion, is so sympathetic that he looks through the doubt, wonder, questions, and fears to the faith that lies directly underneath that pile. Know this: through uncertain and rough times we will juggle both faith and doubt. The important thing is to keep a measure of belief active in the equation.

The Absence of the Algebraic Formula

One of the pastors of a church I attended years ago once told me that his view of the Christian faith was similar to the mathematical equation A + B = C. For example, if you never broke any of the Ten Commandments; if you didn't drink, smoke, swear, or have lusty thoughts; if you went to church every Sunday; if you were involved in a handful of extracurricular church activities; and so on, then you would be blessed, you would have God's approval, and all your prayers would be answered in the positive. It sounds pretty good, doesn't it? I had thought like that much of my life.

When I started cleaning up a financial disaster I had created out of nothing but sheer stupidity and greed, I couldn't afford to tithe. Tithing is a touchy subject, and the church I was attending placed a huge emphasis on giving God 10 percent of your income. Personally, I do think it's a great principle to follow, but back then I didn't have 10 percent to give. I wondered if maybe God wanted me to give up eating or not pay my rent and risk eviction in order to tithe whatever little I had. I remember the nights I tossed and turned and the number of desperate phone calls I made to my older brother for his advice. I sobbed uncontrollably, the type of sobs where your shoulders shake like maracas and your cries sound asthmatic. I experienced minor panic attacks mulling over the issue of whether to tithe. I was convinced that if I didn't tithe, God would punish me by digging my financial grave even further down than the vast pit I was in.

Some people in my life shook their heads in displeasure when I reached my final compromise with God: to give him about five bucks a month. They had pointed their accusatory fingers at me and warned that I had no faith and should quickly gain some in order to tithe the expected 10 percent. Their reasoning was simple: tithe and you will be blessed a hundred times over. Don't tithe and you risk the wrath of a God who thinks of you as a dummy for getting yourself into such a mess and who has no reservations about crushing you in the palm of his hands. Those admonishments didn't help matters, and I continued to wrestle with my decision until a lightbulb flashed in my heart. Eventually I became settled by God's peace in the core of my soul. I was absolutely comfortable with the choice I made and didn't have to worry about his rebuke or disapproval. He wouldn't not bless me financially just because money was tight and I had to cut every corner just to survive. God would still love me and he would still work in my life. Was this $A + B = C$? Nope. More like $A / B - C2 + F1 =$ Who knows?

A formulaic religion is not true spirituality. We can always do the right thing in every circumstance and still be suckerpunched by a life disaster or undergo some type of trouble. We can pray perfectly, with eloquence, and using the right words, yet our prayers just may not get answered. Now, I'm not saying we shouldn't live by a moral compass or live life right; I'm just saying that being a perfect Christian, which isn't even possible, will not guarantee a perfect life. Righteous behavior doesn't always produce blessing in terms of financial, emotional, and mental prosperity. Why? Because none of us are righteous. Our good character is referred to in the Bible as filthy rags. I know many people of faith who walk almost blameless before God and yet suffer some terrible things. Are they not doing something right? Do they not have any faith? Or is it just life?

What happens when the weight of reality crushes the weight of our created absolutes? While I confidently believe in the Bible and in God's promises, I know that life happens. And sometimes it happens with such a seemingly reckless force that we are left to wonder what the heck we've done wrong or how God can be so unfair, so silent, and even so useless in our lives. Paul writes in 1 Corinthians 13:12, "Now we see things imperfectly as in a cloudy mirror, but then we will see everything with perfect clarity." There are things we won't know, reasons we will not understand, and situations that will leave us with more questions than answers. That doesn't mean we need to abandon our faith because we don't get our way. It just means we need to hold on to it longer, because having faith solidifies the presence of God in our lives . . . even if we can't feel it.

Sometimes I wonder what I have faith in and why. I understand that some of my beliefs may change, some of them may lessen, and others may deepen. I know that my beliefs, however strong, will not grant me a magic carpet ride. But I believe, nonetheless.

I have faith in the inherent goodness in people. I have faith in the power of mercy, the strength of dreams, and the unavoidable angst of the unknown. I have faith that they that sow in tears shall reap in laughter. I have faith that the algebraic formula for life doesn't exist—that what we think we want may not be what we necessarily need; that the highways which we are certain will lead us on our journeys just might keep us traveling in the wrong direction. I have faith in the power of possibility, that waking up miserable on a dismal Monday morning may leave our heads on the pillow that same night spinning with ecstasy, love, joy, and comfort. Most importantly, I have faith in God—that he has heard my utterances and that his hands stretch out toward me in mercy for the sole reason that he *is* love. I have faith that all things work together for the good and that the garbage we may have sown in our lives can mysteriously transform into treasures. I have these beliefs merely because it is more difficult for me not to. And I believe that is the crux of why we all believe— because we cannot *not* believe.

In the fifth chapter of Luke, Jesus is preaching near the Sea of Galilee and sees Peter's fishing boat. Peter has been fishing all day and catching zilch. Jesus tells him to throw his net out into the water . . . again. I'm sure Peter is thinking, "You've got to be kidding me! I've been doing it all day, and you're telling me to try one more time? Come on!" But whatever it is that he is thinking, he responds, "If you say so, I'll let the nets down again" (see v. 5). What did Peter have to go on to guarantee a net of slimy fish? Nothing at all. Jesus wasn't a fishing guru; he was a carpenter. But Peter obliged, holding on to the net with both hands and holding on to possibility with his heart. "Just maybe," Peter may have thought, "just maybe I'll get my fish."

He does.

What is our guarantee for belief? For Christians, it is that God hears us, that he has promised never to leave nor forsake us, and that we can find an everlasting peace that passes our understanding. For the agnostics or atheists, the guarantee is that their faith in something—whether family, friends, earth, or humanity—still keeps them holding on to hope somehow.

Faith means hanging around, not giving up on the miracle that may come, not leaving before we may hear a knock at the door. Some miracles come and others never show up. Some prayers are answered, and some are followed by silence. The point of faith is to keep on keeping on. It gives us the right amount of strength to do so.

Without faith, there is no hope; without hope, there is no life. In my own experience, not everything has panned out according to my prayer lists, my dreams, or my childlike demands. I have on many occasions unsteadily walked the thin line of abandoning my faith, but I never have. I don't want to miss out on what I would miss out on if I had no faith.

5

When It Gets Too Loud to Hear

An inability to stay quiet is one of the most conspicuous failings of mankind.

Walter Bagehot

Many reasons lie behind the statements I often hear from other people and even have said myself many times: "I can't hear God." "He is not saying anything." "He is ignoring me." One explanation for why this happens is simply that we aren't listening. Now before you start cursing me out or throwing rotten fruit my way, remember: I said there are *many* reasons we don't hear God. Sometimes we're not listening. Sometimes we're too busy. Sometimes we want to hear God through method A, while God wants to speak to us using method F. And sometimes—and this is probably the most difficult pill to swallow—God isn't saying anything for reasons we, unfortunately, do not know and might never know.

I really feel compassion for the folks who are experiencing their season of silence from God either as it concerns a particular issue or as it concerns their lives. This can be a heavy cross to bear, but it is definitely not something that is out of the ordinary. When Job was scratching himself silly and drowning in grief from the devastating loss of his family, God kept his mouth shut. He didn't utter a word either to comfort Job or to offer him some wisdom during his trial and tribulation period.

In Psalm 22, King David writes, "My God, my God, why have you abandoned me? Why are you so far away when I groan for help? Every day I call to you, my God, but you do not answer. Every night you hear my voice, but I find no relief" (Ps. 22:1–2). This psalm is often compared to the words Jesus spoke when he hung on the cross on the brink of death. As he toiled between fighting for his life and surrendering to death, Jesus cried out, "My God, my God, why have you abandoned me?" (Matt. 27:46). God kept his mouth shut and did not utter a word.

Did you know that God was silent for four hundred years from the time the last word of the Old Testament book Malachi was written to the day the birth of Jesus was recorded? God wasn't staring into space twirling his hair around his finger for four centuries, but neither did he open his mouth.

As I've said before, the silence of God doesn't indicate his absence. It just means he is not saying anything. In these moments we cannot perform any tricks or stunts or use any manipulative strategies to make him pipe up. He has his reasons. We don't know what they are, but he still loves us and is working in our lives during this time. This is something we ought never to forget.

I try to be very careful about giving advice to someone whose fervent prayers seem to fall on deaf ears or whose knocks on heaven's door just give them sore and bruised knuckles and, of course, no reply like, "Hi there! How can I help you?" I definitely don't tell people that they need to try harder or pray louder or use fancier words or pray in the early hours of dawn and on their knees, banging their heads on the floor.

We often give that kind of advice to those around us who are struggling with spiritual issues. We become experts at figuring out God and faith, and we somehow believe we are able to see with such clarity the answers to questions that just might not have any answers. Let me give you a fictitious example. Johnny is frustrated and depressed because God is silent in his spiritual walk. Instead of encouraging him just to walk through the muck for the season, his brother David tells him he is doing something wrong. "Stop sinning," David tells Johnny. "Stop doing this and stop doing that. God always speaks to good people who do good things all the time."

Another friend, Suzy, comes along and tells David that he is not praying enough, that he should go to church on Sundays *and* on Wednesdays, and that he should maybe even lead a small group. Suzy says, "David, if you work hard enough and do all these things, God is definitely going to notice and start communicating to you." (If you read the book of Job, you'll find these same types of characters doing the same thing to Job.) Poor Johnny. The only thing their foolish suggestions do is make him more frustrated and more depressed.

Think about this for a minute. Are we too insecure or too weak or too scared to admit the reality that sometimes God is silent? That maybe that's not such of a bad thing? That maybe it can act as a pretty accurate barometer of whether we really have faith in God? Or do we just believe him when everything is dandy and he seems to be whispering sweet nothings in our ears every two seconds? If you are experiencing God's silence right now, maybe, just maybe it has nothing to do with what you are doing or not doing. Endure it. Walk through it. Don't give up talking to God. Don't give up believing that he is active though hidden or present though silent.

But you know what else? Sometimes we are the answer to God's silence. Sometimes it does have to do with us. Sometimes we are a little too loud for God to get through. I'm not going to point a finger at your situation and try to figure out where you stand in the whole scheme of things. This is a great opportunity for you to experience true spiritual reflection and meditation. This is where you need to be honest with yourself, think on your own, and quiet down to see if you are getting in the way of God's tidings.

The Problem with Being Quiet

Prayer can be an equally spiritually rewarding and frustrating experience. It's a great time to purge ourselves of needs, wants, and feelings, as well as to spend time reflecting on our inner self and on God. It's also probably the primary opportunity to intentionally hear God's voice deep down in our spirits. If we're honest with ourselves, however, most of us probably spend most of our prayer time in vocal clearance of whatever is burdening our hearts and our minds. We pray for financial stability, we pray for the poor, we pray for the safety of our children, we pray for good health, we pray for wisdom to make the right decisions, we pray for our neighbors, we pray for ourselves. Yada, yada, yada. We pray about anything, really, for which we need immediate and divine intervention.

Then there is this block of time in prayer where we are supposed to be quiet and just rest in the presence of the Eternal and, in a way I can't quite describe or explain, listen for the voice of God. I don't know many people who practice this on a regular basis. We are much better at being Chatty Cathys. We are much better at whipping out and numbly reciting our mile-long prayer lists with legitimate and—let's get real— not-so-legitimate requests. We are much better at letting out a big sigh of "amen" at the end of our gimmie-gimmie-gimmie soliloquies and resuming our fast-paced lives, jetting forward with whatever we have to do at full speed.

But to sit there during our time of reflection and allot five minutes or so to doing nothing except being still and quiet? Isn't that kind of hard to do? How do you shut your brain off? How do you turn down the volume of your pain, frustration, heartaches, and fears? And isn't not doing or not saying anything a complete waste of time? I'm sure all of us could use that five, ten, or fifteen minutes doing something more productive, like replying to our backed-up emails, or cleaning out our car, or putting in more time telling God what's going on in our lives, as if he doesn't already know.

Being still and listening for God can seem just as easy as crossing the Sahara Desert wearing a snowsuit and no shoes. I admire people who meditate on a regular basis. They have learned how to quiet themselves, how to shut down the forces around them that vie for their attention, and how to rest in nothingness. They know how to free their mind of everything that is unnecessary, which, during meditation, is pretty much everything.

I truly consider it a miracle if I'm able to sit still and clear my brain for more than two minutes. This has been a work in progress for me for quite some time, and I'm not ashamed to say it's still a struggle. I have tried incorporating stillness in my prayer time, and most of my attempts have been largely unsuccessful. The first few times the routine was the same. I set my alarm for five minutes. What's five minutes of quiet, right? It should be a walk in the park. I took some deep breaths, closed my eyes, and crossed my legs. So far ten seconds had passed. Then I started thinking about how exactly I was supposed to think about nothing except trying to think about nothing and, hopefully, hear some stirrings from God. Thirty seconds. "Stop thinking!" I silently yelled to myself.

Then, out of the clear blue at around minute one, I started remembering and thinking about the strangest of things. It's amazing what runs through your mind when you give it an empty slot of time. Your mind starts running wild. My thoughts were consumed with the oddest of things. "How much calcium do I really need?" "Remember the time during my violin lesson when I told my teacher that all my mom does all day is sit around and eat watermelon and gossip with her sister?" "Is Splenda really bad for you?" Two and a half minutes had passed. I screamed to myself, "Shut up already!"

Get my drift? My brain is constantly in motion, not unlike yours, I'm sure. As a writer, I spend a lot of time thinking, creating, imagining, and paying attention to different things every minute of my waking day. I never slow down. I don't have an emergency valve to press that will shut my brain off.

I bet you anything being quiet before God is a challenge for you as well. Is this because we are so overwhelmed by the stuff that is happening in our lives that we feel it is important for us to get every word in edgewise that we can within a specific time frame or God won't know how to help us out? Is being quiet boring? Or do we not think that our quiet can create an environment where we can be more aware of God's thoughts because we are not blabbing away ourselves? Do we not think that he will speak to us, and so we think, "Why bother sitting there staring into space when I'm not going to get anything out of it anyway?" What I believe happens most times is that our minds become more cluttered than our grandmother's attic. This makes it almost impossible to be still and silent. On one hand, if we want to hear God badly enough, our souls become especially frenzied and desperate to hear him. Our eyes are shut so tightly that Botox wouldn't stand a chance at eliminating the wrinkles that have accumulated around our peepers. It's almost as if we're subconsciously repeating this mantra: "God *will* speak to me. God *will* speak to me. God *will* speak to me." But sometimes all that does is generate such a distressing level of anguish that we become too focused on that particular want instead of being content just sitting in silence. Instead of allowing God to take the wheel of our time of reflection and prayer and synthesize what he knows we need with what we're asking for, we just want him to open his mouth already and start saying something. You know what? If he did speak, chances are we probably wouldn't hear him anyway because our need is too loud.

Can we hear God in our hearts? Sure. Should we use part of our prayer time in silence to maybe position ourselves to be in a better place of listening? Absolutely. Should we be so desperate that we demand he speak? No. Doing that just takes the wonder, beauty, and magic out of the whole spirituality thing. We need to let God be God and stop laying down the law that he do something within the time period we have impatiently and brashly extended him.

On the other hand, sometimes during this period of meditation, we can't hear God because we have so much on our minds—most of which I refer to affectionately as junk. We have a lot of stuff—worries, questions, ideas, problems, feelings, thoughts—occupying a lot of space in our hearts and minds. This can make listening almost impossible. I have found this to be one of my problems.

Daily life with its daily routine can almost act like a hazard. We are bogged down by so many different things. When is my tax refund coming? Why am I losing my hair? Will I ever get married? Should I put my ailing mother in a nursing home? Will I ever get pregnant? Will I get a job? Will I ever sell this house? How can I afford my son's leukemia treatment?

With the need to stay quiet and the amount of thoughts that concurrently consume our minds, I suppose this is where practice makes perfect. Quieting our inner dialogue and being still is definitely a good habit to have. Yet it doesn't come so easily or so quickly for most of us. This doesn't mean we need to stop trying. This doesn't mean we need to give up shutting our minds off or even just lowering the volume a little. It simply means we need to accept the challenge and keep at it so we get better.

I remember when I had just moved to Nashville and started working out for the first time in my entire life. I was twenty-two years old, and the only exercise I'd ever done was whatever the teachers wanted me to do in elementary school gym class. Well, I did briefly attempt a shot at physical activity when I was sixteen. But that was because I was madly in love with one of my older brother's friends, a very athletic kind of guy, and wanted to impress him. My brother and the love of my life had been hanging out at our house and were on their way out to see a movie or something. I had an idea to attract his attention in a positive way.

I threw on a pair of shorts and a big T-shirt to cover my flabby and chubby body and found a pair of old running shoes to put on. Actually, they were a pair of flimsy Keds. Who was I kidding? I didn't have any type of sneaker that had anything to do with running. As the two guys were getting ready to leave, I brushed past them and put on my best "game" face. I winked at my love and blurted out, "See ya. Goin' for a run." My brother smirked and rolled his eyes, but I'm pretty sure I got a look of approval from my crush.

I bolted out the front doors and started pounding my feet on the pavement. By the time I ran past the third house on my block, I was gasping for breath and felt like my lungs were about to explode. Just then their car passed me on my right, and I waved at the sound of the car horn. I had already forgotten how madly in love I was with the guy who was sitting in the passenger seat. I was trying to breathe without puking. As soon as the car became a tiny dot on the horizon of our neighborhood, I stopped running and walked home, pretty certain I would die. I didn't work out again until about eight years later.

When I eventually started an exercise program, I got smart about it. I realized I didn't have to begin my new journey into health by running a marathon (or even running, period). I could start off slowly and progress into becoming an "elite athlete." I started off exercising ten minutes one day, twenty minutes the next, and so on. And I got better and gained more stamina and strength the longer and harder I worked at it.

This example is an obvious parallel, of course, to working on becoming still in our spirits, but it goes without saying that learning to tune ourselves out and focus in on God demands work, time, and energy. No one said that quieting our minds would be easy, but I believe if we spent more time at least trying, we'd catch a few surprises from God along the way.

The Martha Syndrome

I've noticed that there are a lot of ragged Christians out in the world. They are tired, burned out, and worn out. A lot of times these people put their hands into a bunch of different service-oriented projects for many reasons. They are on the boards of eight different groups. They volunteer for three different organizations five times a week. They are in charge of the bake sale, the church library, and the community reading program. They not only take care of their own four kids but eagerly volunteer to babysit the kids in the neighborhood every Tuesday. They sing in the choir, they play the trumpet in the band, and they mentor four underprivileged kids. Some of these people do it from the bottom of their hearts. Others do it because they think they have to. And some do it because they think it will earn them some brownie points, either from God or from leaders in the church or community.

Nothing is wrong with serving or doing something other than focusing on caring for yourself and your own needs. Nothing is wrong with volunteering or helping others who need your help. However, there is a problem when we stretch ourselves too thin and focus solely on what we need to get done and so then forget about our spiritual needs. Somehow we think we have too much to do to pray, to meditate, and to be still. Whatever time we have must be put toward checking off the hundred things we have written down on our task list. Spiritual time? Gimme a break. Not enough hours in the day for that. The perfect time for anything spiritually oriented is on Sunday mornings when we go to church or during any other time we do something religious as a community.

When we put spirituality on the back burner and forget we need to be nurturing our spirits the same way we need to work out our physical bodies, we become legalistic. Our religion becomes nothing more than something we practice once a week out of habit. When we invest ourselves only in doing "stuff" instead of in prayer and contemplation, our passion for the inner life and for God fades.

We are all guilty of exchanging personal spirituality for busy service. Meditation for activity. Mystery for to-do lists. We must find some sort of balance. Certainly, we all cannot be so ethereal in our lives that we never do laundry, or go to work, or care for our kids or spouse. But I think many people in this world don't make spiritual matters a priority, and that is why they wonder where God is or why they haven't felt him in ages.

In the Gospel of Luke, the writer tells a short story about two sisters who are preparing dinner for Jesus and his disciples:

> As Jesus and the disciples continued on their way to Jerusalem, they came to a certain village where a woman named Martha welcomed him into her home. Her sister, Mary, sat at the Lord's feet, listening to what he taught. But Martha was distracted by the big dinner she was preparing. She came to Jesus and said, "Lord, doesn't it seem unfair to you that my sister just sits here while I do all the work? Tell her to come and help me." But the Lord said to her, "My dear Martha, you are worried and upset over all these details! There is only one thing worth being concerned about. Mary has discovered it, and it will not be taken away from her."
>
> Luke 10:38–42

Martha was the older, more responsible sister who undoubtedly ran a tight ship in her household. She worked hard to make sure the dishes were always washed, the laundry was always done, the guest bathroom had fresh towels, and the refrigerator was full of plenty of food that could be whipped up into a gourmet feast at a moment's notice. These are such wonderful traits to have. Martha was organized, paid attention to details, was efficient, and always stayed on top of things. In walked her younger sister, Mary, who was probably less of all these things, and started spiritually swooning at this visiting teacher instead of playing the role of Martha's assistant in the kitchen.

Martha obviously needed help, and Mary was too busy searching out the deep things of her life and this world. Martha had every right to get upset, but Jesus assuaged her violent outburst and told her to relax and take it easy for a bit. Jesus was saying something like, "Who cares if the bread doesn't rise perfectly, or that the silverware isn't so polished, or that the glasses are mismatched, or that the chicken needs more salt? Who cares if the dishwasher hasn't been unloaded yet, or if you don't have the right side dish, or if the table hasn't been Pledged spotless? I am not here to be served; I'm here so you can learn of me. And all these details you are consumed with are making you tired, frustrated, and judgmental of other people. All this wasted energy is not doing one ounce of good in the matters which concern your heart and your spirit."

And to us today, Jesus is saying something similar. "Who cares if you haven't cleaned out your attic in five years? You also haven't sat down and talked to me in three weeks." "Who cares if you don't match up with the Joneses? When was the last time you took stock of why you are allowing your superficial obsessions to negatively impact your relationship with your wife and your kids?" "Who cares if you can't make church on Sunday or Bible study on Wednesday? Maybe you should start caring about spending more time with me on Mondays through Saturdays."

We can all suffer the Martha syndrome in our lives. We get busy with so many different things and so many different people that pull us in every direction. It's easy to justify spending less time watering our spiritual lives because we have a husband and four kids and a home and a part-time job to worry about. But you know what the reality is? Not spending time with God will not make things easier on us or give us an extra hour every day. And it definitely will not afford him the space to weave purpose into our lives.

Before you start accusing God of being the Invisible Man, how much of your energy is focused on your faith walk? Do you prefer to do stuff to prove the legitimacy of your faith, or is resting in him enough to give you peace? It's important that we strive to find a balance between Martha and Mary. Both women have great qualities we can learn from. Still, Mary had a deep understanding that spirituality was an important, if not the most important, part of her life. We can't expect God to pull out all the stops in our lives if we don't let him. It wouldn't hurt us to take a break from the busy and talk to him every now and then.

Don't just go to church because you should do it and you teach Sunday school. Do it because you really love it and have your own personal faith journey that you are constantly investing in. Don't just sing in the choir every weekend because you're afraid to be called lazy or uncommitted if you don't. Do it because it means something deep to you, and make sure you take the time during the weekdays to commune with God so the words you sing mean more than something that sounds pretty. Don't just lead youth group because your pastor told you that you should. Do it because you realize that young people need to know why faith matters and you have a longing in your heart to help them on their journey.

Open Mouth, Insert Foot

I talk a lot. There, I said it. It has to do with the fact that during the day, I'm alone most of the time. I work from home, so I don't have a whole lot of opportunity to engage in conversation throughout the day. The minute I get on the phone with a friend or have dinner with some folks, my blabbermouth opens, and it can take the weight of a sumo wrestler to squeeze it shut, especially after a glass or two of wine. I have unintentionally offended people, shared things about myself that I would have rather not shared, and honestly just looked stupid. And after a few foot-in-the-mouth episodes where it definitely would have been to my advantage to shut up, I started becoming more conscious of talking so much.

Sometimes I think my mouth is like a vacuum, sucking in other people's energies and aborting any opportunity for them to say something or, more importantly, for me to hear something they want to share. I do the same thing with God. I babble. I rant. I rave. I repeat things. I constantly speckle my talks with him with "Whys?" and "What ifs?" and then shamelessly answer my own questions a thousand different ways. Every once in a while, I know I'm crossing the line. I feel like God wants to grab me by my shoulders, shake me, and say, "My goodness, woman. Can you just be silent for one minute? I'm trying to tell you something, but you are spurting out nonsense. Shush already."

Now, God is delighted to listen to our prayers, and he is even more thrilled that we are coming to him in the first place. Our stutters, stammers, and blubbering messes are not things that repulse him or make him want to throw some cotton balls in his ears. Yet I think that we can go overboard with our dialogue and completely miss what he wants to say to us. We can talk too much, or get off track, or be so consumed by the utterly fascinating comments and suggestions we have that even if he was speaking to us with a bullhorn, we couldn't possibly hear him.

I'm reminded of Peter, one of Jesus's disciples. He was a bold, brash, rough-around-the-edges type of guy. He frequently suffered from the habit of speaking without thinking first—foot-in-mouth disease. The Bible records an event where Jesus had taken Peter and two other men with him to pray on top of a mountain. In the middle of the prayer session, the three men fell into a deep sleep. Only Jesus remained awake.

As he prayed and the three men snored on top of that peak with the wind blowing over their faces, Jesus began to undergo a supernatural transformation that is probably difficult for many of us to picture. His body dissolved and he turned into a spirit, a glowing white light. At the same time, the ghosts of Elijah and Moses appeared before him, and the three spiritual leaders engaged in a conversation, though we don't know what was said. However, this exchange was so brilliant, moving, and powerful that the three disciples woke up from their nap. Their mouths dropped to the ground in astonishment because of what they saw when they rubbed the sleep out of their eyes. Before they had an opportunity to question whether they were dreaming, the silhouettes of Moses and Elijah slowly started to disappear. Peter, anxious not to let an opportunity to utter words of brilliance go by, blurted out, "Master, it's wonderful for us to be here! Let's make three shelters as memorials—one for you, one for Moses, and one for Elijah" (Luke 9:33).

Imagine that. Two prophets who lived centuries earlier, whose life-changing stories were still told hundreds of generations later, and who miraculously appeared out of thin air, are interrupted by a bumbling fool. Never mind that this was an episode that spoke of the supernatural. Never mind that this was a display of God unfolding mystery in front of mere mortals. Never mind that just minutes before, Peter was too tired to stay awake for prayer and didn't even get to the beginning "Dear Lord" part before he was conked out. Peter doesn't even think about these things.

He was an opportunist (which is not a bad thing) and simply decided that the appearance of Moses and Elijah demanded the building of memorials to celebrate the occasion. "Hey, dudes, don't go anywhere yet," Peter interjected. "I'm thinking we should start a building fund and get the ball rolling on creating some real modern, contemporary tabernacles for you guys. Maybe we can use the same model for each, or we could create different ones to show your different personalities. As a matter of fact, John here has some tools down below the mountain. I can go grab them and see what I can do. What do you think?"

The Bible tells us that while he chattered on and on, a cloud covered all the men who rested on that mountain, and they were all struck with fear. In a booming voice from this cloud, God interrupted Peter and said, "This is my Son, my Chosen One. Listen to him" (Luke 9:35). In other words, "Peter, shut up. This is not about you. This is not about your ideas. This is not about your plans. This is about faith. This is about my Son. And this is about the fate of the world. Stop your blubbering and start listening."

Are we directing all of our energies, thoughts, and verbiage to what we desperately want to say instead of paying attention to God? Are we using too many words and not stilling our souls, the place where words don't have to be spoken and where the conduit lies to connect ourselves to God? Do we feel that we owe God the privilege of hearing our ideas or our commentary on certain things instead of perhaps asking what ideas or commentaries God wants to shift our way?

We all have moments when we are guilty of not allowing God to be God and do his thing because we have cluttered our minds and hearts with everything under the sun. God is not so unaware that he doesn't know what we need or want, or what our fears are, or what kind of miracle we need to come our way. Sometimes we keep running our mouths because we are afraid God is not going to remember all of the needs in our lives. God doesn't forget. He doesn't have amnesia or suffer from short-term memory loss. Nor does he not remember anything unless he writes it down. God is able and willing to commune with us in different ways, especially in prayer. This is where we need to crack open the window or door of our lives to make a way for him.

Stop thinking so much. Stop talking so much. Stop worrying so much. Stop getting distracted so much. Sure, I know these things are difficult to execute, but if you focus on lessening the parts of you that rob the time where God mandates a quiet spirit, you will be more apt to experience peace and, of course, a word or two deep in your spirit from none other than the "big man upstairs."

6

Seeing the Invisible through the Visible

I hear and behold God in every object . . .
Why should I wish to see God better than this day?
I see something of God each hour of the twenty four,
   and each moment then,
In the faces of men and women I see God, and in my
   own face in the glass.

                                    Walt Whitman

It is easy to find the presence of God or even a glimpse of
his silhouette through the beauty of nature and creation.
If you stand on top of a mountain peak (and I'm not just
talking about Mount Kilimanjaro here), it's hard not to believe divine hands crafted what greets your eyes—a pristine,
postcard-perfect landscape. It's hard not to believe that even

in the middle of the chaos and heartache of life, there is a deity beyond eternity and our comprehension that carved out scenic mountain ranges sprinkled with soft white snow, roaring white-water rivers slicing between rugged canyons, and green rolling hills bursting with radiant sunflowers that sway in a breeze that seems to lovingly whisper your name.

I'm sure most of you can sense a nudge of the divine when put your life on pause and take a few minutes to admire the unique aesthetics of Mother Nature. From a bubbling brook that flows in your backyard, to a blooming rose in a barren desert, to a midnight black sky adorned with twinkly stars, to a transparent ocean showing off neon-colored life forms that look more like aliens than plants or animals—there is something so distinctive, unbelievable, and magical about nature and its design that it's almost impossible to think it just randomly erupted from a cosmic boom. I'm a sucker for shows on the National Geographic Channel or Discovery Channel that narrate detailed commentaries about the intricacies of plant and animal life. I always watch the ending credits, muttering under my breath, "How can I not believe in God?"

But as wonderful and as complex as nature is, and as viable as I believe it is as an evidence of our Creator, I gotta be honest. A brilliant bouquet of daises is probably not going to make my breaking heart stop breaking. Gazing wide-eyed at dolphins diving in the middle of the azure, glistening Caribbean Sea is probably not going to cure my depression. Gaping in wonder at a solar eclipse is probably not going to be my road to belief when I start doubting God.

Here is where another piece of God's creation steps in. After God molded the universe; hung the stars and planets in space; adorned the earth with oceans, mountains, deserts, and valleys; and threw in a couple of lions, tigers, and bears, he paused. He thought for a few minutes. "This is good stuff. It's beautiful. I like it." And then he sensed a missing link. Human beings. Masses of flesh, blood, bone, and tissue with unique personalities and the ability to think, love, feel, and act for themselves.

Humanity was God's gift to the world, a created image of himself. Relationships are critical components of our lives. They help us understand humanity. They help us practice grace. They help us grow. They help us be better people. They provide for us a net of comfort and care when we need it. In that regard, relationships hold a lot of value even in spite of certain challenges. For instance, some ties can bind best friends for life even if they have totally different backgrounds, life experiences, and political views and even if distance separates them. There is even the powerful dynamic of strangers who perform, even unknowingly, random acts of kindness that can actually turn our day around for the better. They are the men and women we pass by on the street on a bleak Tuesday morning who we will probably never see again but who in an instant brighten our otherwise depressing morning with their sincere, multi-million-dollar smile.

We may never be able to draw the face of God like a police sketch artist, because, quite frankly, we have no idea what he looks like. We may never be able to officially prove his existence in the heavens above. We may feel, at times, his absence more than his presence. We may feel a sense of abandonment from him when times get rough. But make no mistake: God made extensions of himself. I have an odd feeling he did this as one way to help us believe he exists.

Yes, I know not everyone is good or kind or faithful. I know you might have coworkers who gossip too much and have hissed mean things about you behind your back. I know wicked people who do unspeakable things roam the earth.

The annals of history are loaded with these folks. I know you might have a father who did things to you that no father should ever be able to even think of doing. I know you might have a spouse who left you for no good reason other than that the nanny had blonder hair, was twenty pounds lighter, and was twenty years younger. People aren't always great, nor do they always do the right thing. Believe me, I understand this. This just speaks of the fact that evil is rampant and we, especially those of us who are attuned to the spiritual world, need to be better at activating and leaving behind a legacy of love, faith, and purpose.

But in the same vein, I like to pay more attention to the people who make a difference in the lives of others in big and small ways. The grocery clerk who tells you every morning how beautiful you are. The mechanic who knows about your financial situation and didn't charge you for the work he did on your transmission. The sister who spent days and nights with you after each chemo treatment you went through. The parent who prayed every single day for you to come back home. God is shining through these hearts, through these faces, and through these active gifts of mercy. It is the divine that is resting in the shadows behind the structures of flesh and bones.

Best-selling author Philip Yancey wrote an article reflecting his thoughts on 9/11. He writes:

> In Washington and Chicago, as I talked about the special edition of *Where Is God When It Hurts?*, inevitably the interviewer would turn the question back on me. "Well, where is God at a time like this?" Sometimes I countered some of the harmful things other Christian spokesmen had said, bringing guilt and judgment to a time that begged for comfort and grace. I talked of Jesus' response to tragedies, especially in Luke 13. And then I told of a man who came up to me one

time and said, "Sorry, I don't have time to read your book. Can you just answer that question for me in a sentence or two?"

I thought for a moment and said, "I guess the answer to that question is another question. Where is the church when it hurts? If the church is doing its job—binding wounds, comforting the grieving, offering food to the hungry—I don't think people will wonder so much where God is when it hurts. They'll know where God is: in the presence of his people on earth."[1]

Divine Evidence through Jars of Clay

We are extensions of God. We are his hands. We are his feet. We are his smile. We are his vessels of mercy, compassion, grace, and love. We are evidence of the divine, even through the obvious fissures of the cracked jars of clay that define our broken nature. Sometimes, though, we do a terrible job at being creatures made in his image.

Some people try their darnedest to believe in God. Others have absolutely no problem believing in the unseen. The sad truth is that some of the latter are the nastiest, most selfish, and most culturally ignorant people on the planet. They devoutly believe in God and practice religion, but their attitude stinks, and you'd never know they are being guided by some form of higher purpose. You know what? Some people who are struggling with faith see them, whether intentionally or not, as a model on which to base their portrait of God. And what do they see? A human being who is the antithesis of the divine.

Is the only point of spirituality to uphold people who believe in God or to pat them on the back for having such a solid faith? I certainly hope not, because in the grand scheme of some believers' ugliness, big deal! I am embarrassed by

111

these kinds of Christians. Instead of being loving, they are spiteful. Instead of showing compassion, they judge. Instead of serving others, they lead with an iron fist. Instead of being kind, they have attitude problems.

I remember when my sister came back from Thailand and got a temporary job as a contractor for a company in North Carolina. She started working with a woman who was obviously a Christian. My sister said that you wouldn't have known it, however, if not for the hundred Bible verse stickers that bedecked almost every inch of her cubicle walls, the Bible verse cartoon calendar propped on her desk, and the large Bible covered by a pastel, flowery cloth bag next to her in-box. Now, if you want to trumpet your faith and if you're proud of what you believe in, by all means, flaunt it. Wear a T-shirt, slap a bumper sticker on your car, do whatever you want to do. But don't call yourself a representative of the "Good News" when you have the world's biggest attitude problem.

My sister would approach this woman to mark up some reports or to gather information together for a specific project. Mind you, these weren't out-of-the-ordinary or time-consuming tasks. The woman would often respond with an exasperated sigh and a very dramatic roll of the eyes. Usually the reply was, "Not right now. I'm busy," and then she'd turn away.

This wasn't a one-time deal, either. It would happen constantly. This woman of "great faith" was always moody, acted as if doing one simple thing was an enormous chore, and made a big stink about being interrupted at work by work-related issues. If we are people who live by faith, is this how we really want to live our lives? By being not-nice people? It's like wearing a "What Would Jesus Do?" bracelet and cursing out the cashier at Burger King because she gave you a Coke instead of a Diet Coke.

For the sake of faith, for the sake of God, and for the sake of love, we must personify God. Not that we don't have bad days, or never slip up, or have to act perfect all the time. But come on now—why can't we act a little nicer to the stranger, to the family member, and to the friend? Why can't we go the extra mile? Why can't we do something extra special for someone just to show that we care? And why can't we just help someone when we have the capacity to do so?

It's easy to be like Jesus when the only people you hang out with go to your church. It's easy to be sweet and kind when you have a small but sweet and kind social circle you don't really venture out of. But it's a big world, people. Just because you don't really talk to your next-door neighbor—the one who has the obnoxiously loud lawn mower and is always dangling a cigarette out of his mouth—doesn't mean he's not there. Just because you ignore the ragged, tired, and worn-out recovering drug addict who spends each morning in the coffee shop doesn't mean she doesn't exist. If we are supposed to be reflections of the divine, visions of the one whom we cannot see, the voice of one who is silent, why do we ignore folks who don't belong to our social circle, who make us uncomfortable, who don't fit in with us, or who may never be able to do anything for us?

This reminds me of the famous parable Jesus told about the Good Samaritan, recorded in Luke 10. A scholar of the Jewish law comes up to Jesus with a specific purpose in mind. He doesn't want to get to know Jesus to see who he really is or to learn something from this obviously very wise man. The Bible tells us this expert of the law approached Jesus to test him (see v. 25). He asks, "What should I do to inherit eternal life?" (v. 25). Jesus responds by reminding him of what Moses had said hundreds of years earlier. A lightbulb goes off in the old scholar's head, and he claps his hands in a grand epiphany and says, "Oh yes, I got it. Now I remember. I must love God with all of my heart, my soul, my strength, and my mind. And I must also love my neighbor as myself" (see v. 27).

"That's it." Jesus nods his head and slaps the guy on the back. "Do these things and life will be yours" (see v. 28). The scholar pauses for an instant, scratches his head, and, flushed with the burning desire to trap Jesus in some way, pretends to be confused. What he really wants to do, of course, is find a loophole out of the whole "love other people" command. "Well, who exactly is my 'neighbor'?" he asks Jesus (see v. 29).

With that question, Jesus launches into a parable about the Good Samaritan, otherwise known as the Good Neighbor. You may very well be familiar with the story. A Jewish man is traveling from the town of Jerusalem to Jericho. On his way, he is viciously jumped by a band of robbers who beat him to a bloody, mangled pulp and steal from him everything he has. This poor man lies in a ditch in the middle of nowhere, half dead and unable to help himself or even cry out for help. After some time passes, a priest who is traveling on the same road stumbles upon the crimson-stained, bruised body. He definitely sees the beat-up man but, without missing a beat in his step, walks around him and continues on his merry way. Many translations say that he even crossed the street to avoid the uncomely sight. A groan is heard from the ditch, and I imagine the injured guy thinks something like, "Help me out, you son of a you-know-what. Please! I know you saw me!"

Some more time passes, and a Levite comes along the same road, whistling and admiring the scenic passage, when he too sees the helpless man lying on the side of the road. He does pretty much the same thing. The Levite looks at the man and immediately decides he doesn't want to have any part of helping the guy out. In a matter of seconds he's thinking things such as, "Well, how can I help? I don't know CPR. I'll probably make things worse," or "What am I going to do, carry him? I wouldn't even know what to do with the guy," or "I'm late as it is for my business luncheon. I'm sure someone else after me will do something." And the Levite turns on his heels and saunters over to his business luncheon. Maybe the image of the man with the blackened eyes, bloodied lips, butchered flesh, and broken limbs sears his conscience an hour later as he dines on a porterhouse steak and sips merlot. Or maybe not.

Finally, a third man walks on the side of the street where the bleeding man lies on the cusp of dying. It is a Samaritan. What was the big deal about a Samaritan stopping to help? Jews hated those folks back then, and vice versa. For many years the two groups of people were divided by great prejudice and conflict. It was similar to the hostility shared between the Tutsis and the Hutus that sparked the Rwandan genocide in 1994.

When the eyes of the Samaritan catch sight of the beaten man, the Samaritan freezes in horror. His unbelief at the gory picture quickly turns into compassion, and then he takes action. The Samaritan cradles the dying man in his arms and lifts him out of the ditch. He takes out some supplies from his backpack and starts to soothe this man's wounds with olive oil. Then he wraps the man's oozing skin with clean bandages and tenderly lifts him onto a donkey. Careful not to hit too many bumps that will exacerbate the pain of the dying man, the Samaritan rides the donkey slowly to a nearby inn. There he pays for a room for the man for a couple of nights and tells the innkeeper, "Let this poor guy stay here for a while and take care of him. If it takes longer than I've paid for, don't worry. I'll foot the bill."

After Jesus is finished telling the story, he turns to the man who asked about the exact definition of the word *neighbor* and says, "So who do you think the neighbor was in this story, buddy?" (see Luke 10:36). The reply is obvious. Before the scholar turns and walks away, Jesus commissions him: "Be that neighbor. Do the same thing. Help others. Be an example" (see Luke 10:37). This was not, of course, the medicine that this teacher of the law necessarily wanted to swallow.

Recently I was watching the news and came across a horrific video that also was blasted all over the Internet. It was surveillance footage that captured a woman, Esmin Green, sitting in an emergency room in a New York hospital. She had been there for about twenty-four hours when, all of a sudden, she fell out of a chair onto her face and started to convulse on the floor. She lay there for an hour before a nurse came by and pronounced the woman dead.

It's sad and tragic, but what's even worse is that in the time from when she collapsed until that nurse came, a handful of hospital workers and even a security officer came by, saw the woman lying on the floor, and simply ignored her and walked away. This happened on at least three separate occasions. Likewise, the patients who sat in the waiting room didn't budge an inch. They simply watched a woman's body writhing on cold, hard linoleum and looked on with apathy as if they were watching a blade of grass grow. Esmin was invisible.

The video is horrible to watch, but it's even more horrible to imagine that people can be so apathetic, so compassionless, and so cruel. In an article on its website, CNN commented, "To people around the world who have seen the video, Esmin Green is a symbol of a health-care system that seems to have failed horribly."[2] I agree with that statement, but I think it's more than just a health care system that screwed up. This incident speaks volumes about how humans don't want to be bothered by things outside of their comfort zone or even their little two-by-four world. Honestly, what is the matter with us? What is so wrong with people in general that we would rather pick our noses and stare blindly into space than ask someone, "Hey, are you okay? Is there anything I can do for you?"

What about Christians? Are we any better than anyone else when a lot of us live in our microcosms, associating only with particular people who look like us, dress like us, smell like us, and spout the same lingo as us? The Bible challenges, "Don't look out only for your own interests, but take an interest in others, too" (Phil. 2:4). If we are supposed to reflect God, most of us need to do a better job. Most of us need to practice more kindness, more patience, more forgiveness, and more love. I know I do, especially in the area of patience.

Who cares how big our Bible is, or how often we go to church, or how many Scriptures we have memorized, or how we don't smoke, drink, do drugs, or say bad words? Have you given to the needy this week? Have you told your mom you love her? Have you told your husband how much you appreciate him? Have you at least once this week asked the bus driver how his morning is? Have you helped carry your eighty-year-old neighbor's grocery bags up to her fifth-floor apartment? Have you hugged a child? Have you offered your home for a passing guest? Have you loved instead of judged? Encouraged instead of gossiped? Forgiven instead of hated? Remember, we just might be the only God people ever see. Don't take it lightly that we are all made in God's image. Let's pay more attention to reflecting that as we go about our days. It just might make a difference in someone else's life.

The Comfort of Friends

When I moved to Nashville from the Northeast in my early twenties, I went through massive culture shock. People talked funny, drove slow, and always sung out "Good mornings" and "How are you's?" Their voices were sugary sweet, the atmosphere of the area was uncomfortably (for me) laid back, and the city was full of gorgeous apartment complexes that were very low priced. It was a beautiful town full of talent, creative energy, and warmth. But I was lonely. I didn't have many friends. I remember being introduced to a young lady a few years younger than me who took me under her wing. She took me to every trendy restaurant and lounge out there. She told me the juicy gossip of the old-money families that paraded around Nashville in their fancy clothes and expensive cars. She showed me parts of the Music City that I never knew existed. But more importantly, she offered me her friendship, which I was forever grateful for.

I was beginning the course of a three-year depression when I met her. It was also a turning point in my faith journey. It was a horrible time, though now I know it was necessary. It was a season when I couldn't feel God. I couldn't hear God. And I definitely couldn't see God. I wrote in my journal when I got home from an evening we shared together just eating pizza, listening to music, and talking. I wrote about our conversations where she also admitted her struggle with faith, where she confessed she also experienced the silent Savior, where she also questioned God. I wrote:

> The gnawing void and pained silence from God that consumed me was soothed by the knowing nod of a friend. We spent the last few hours of a Sunday doing nothing more than expressing hidden emotions that, for whatever reason, we could never express before. I discovered I wasn't the only

one who encountered the emptiness from the silent Savior. I wasn't the only one who had desperate pleas for something to prove God is out there, that he loves me, and that he does have a unique plan for my life. I wasn't the only one who begged for a sign, something that hits you on the head like a ton of bricks. We half-jokingly prayed for the audibility of God's voice many times in our own lives. But that request pushed aside, what we both really wanted was a genuine rendezvous with the one we hoped loved us without fail. Whose love could not be added to or subtracted as a result of anything we did or didn't do. A love that was constant and secure.

Sitting here now, I have a smile on my face because of the irony. Earlier this morning, I had bled lonely tears. I questioned the decisions I made. I had even hated myself for these things, but now a bright smile lights up my face. Many times I pleaded with God to [let me] feel his warm embrace around me. I never have. And maybe I never will. But what he has taught me (at least I think, because I can't technically hear him) is that he gave me a hug today through a friend. He gave me comfort today through a friend. He gave me peace today through a friend. He showed up today through a friend.

Surely if God created human beings in his likeness, we can be mirrors of his goodness. He can use others and even use us to show that he is real. This is a lesson for all of us to learn about how to both be a good friend and also accept friendship and lean on people when the going gets tough. How many of us really invest in the lives of others? How much time do we take out of our day to encourage someone, or ask how they are, or show some genuine concern because they haven't been around much? How often do we forgo the small talk that sometimes just gets people nowhere and instead start getting authentic with one another? How do we care for and maintain our friendships?

We're all busy people. I don't know one friend or acquaintance who does nothing all day but sit in the sun and read a book. Everybody I know has a demanding job, or kids, or a spouse, or sick people they have to care for, or degrees they need to finish, or housework that needs to get done, or businesses to start, or books or songs to write. In the middle of our jam-packed schedules, we just might forget that we need a friend or that we need to be a friend.

Proverbs tells us, "The heartfelt counsel of a friend is as sweet as perfume and incense" (27:9). Certainly when we are questioning major decisions or life events that will take us to different places in our lives, those who know us on such a deep level can offer us wisdom in these moments, even when God may not be giving us a clear picture. Don't misunderstand me. I'm not saying we should substitute our friends for God; I just believe he gave us these gifts as a supplement. As an accompaniment to what could be a very boring and very lonely life. As a loving nudge when we want to give up. As a source of prayer.

God in Prayer

The divine can work through us in the lives of other people by prayer. I often talk about how important prayer is, especially praying for other people. I don't know how it all really works, how exactly you ask and how and when and even if you receive; I just know that prayer can bring about change and transformation in our lives. Whether we are battling the intricacies of faith, or have some serious things standing in the way of our belief, or especially if God is pretty much "mum" in our lives, the prayers of other people just may help to unravel the knots in our bellies and keep us plugging along.

A family member of mine used to scoff at asking people for prayer. "Why bother?" she used to tell me. "All people are really interested in is finding out ugly stuff about you. Just pray on your own and keep your dirty laundry to yourself." Hmmm. On the one hand, that can be true. There are plenty of insincere and nosey folks out there who care more about your problems than helping you find some divine guidance to lead you on your way.

And certainly there are some private and personal issues that not everyone needs to know about. You don't have to be so vulnerable with people at times if you don't feel comfortable. I've had a handful of moments when I couldn't ask for prayer for a particular situation because I wasn't ready to share my most personal matters of the heart—matters that I myself was having trouble accepting.

And there are especially some things you may be struggling with that you should do your own homework on or deal with head-on before you ask for prayer. If you are having problems with your husband, for example, and haven't tried to iron out the differences or come to some agreement with him, don't bother running to your small group to have them lay hands on you. It would be foolish. I think that's just a way of not dealing with your problem and of using people or prayer as a Band-Aid. It would serve you better to talk to your husband first and take things from there.

On the other hand, sometimes we unintentionally hurt ourselves and even our spirituality or peace of mind by being defensive and not risking being emotionally open to those who are dear to our hearts. I have a few close friends. I'm very choosy about whom I let into my "best friend" circle for various reasons. But even from them, with the exception of one or two of my best friends, I have often hidden certain aspects of my life for fear of what they would think or say. I think I have to be perfect or at least seem perfect on a superficial level. I have determined that if they knew the mistakes I had made or my poor judgment, their image of me would be shattered. Crushed. Demolished. And things would change. I would be looked at as stupid, foolish, uncertain, flippant, or a flip-flopper.

I remember going to lunch once with my friend Nichole. We had recently connected and found out we had a lot in common. I picked her up from work one day, and as we sat outside a gorgeous café enjoying delectable food and soaking in the glorious sunlight, I felt nudged in my heart. Our conversation turned to very deep matters, and we each began to share our past. I wanted so desperately to tell her certain things that weighed on my heart like an anchor on an ant. My first impression was to keep my mouth shut. "Don't say a word," I warned myself. "She will see you in a different light . . . a horrible light like the ones in department store dressing rooms where every flaw and every imperfection is illuminated to a remarkable and scary degree."

I opted to ignore my thoughts, however, and I am so grateful I did. I purged stuff to her that I had not told a soul. Guess what happened? She was so kind and so appreciative that I had trusted her enough to get down and dirty. She offered me great advice, sincerely told me she would keep me in her prayers, and helped to calm a lot of my anxiety. Ever since that time, we have both confided equally in each other and have exercised our friendship in praying for one another—for whatever, whenever, at all hours of the day.

Praying for people is important because it helps them on their spiritual and life journey. When our friends are weak and cannot pray for themselves, we can be the channel through which God works in their lives, as I have experienced and seen evidenced in my friends. This is not to say that God won't show up, respond to their call, fill their needs, or make his presence known without their uttered words. This just means we can supplement their faith, and we can believe that their lives can be touched or their needs met in some way. Sometimes we can't see God in our own lives and are too tired to keep trying. How lucky we are to have people around us who care enough and love us enough to help us get to a place where we can keep trying.

When someone—whether a loved one, an acquaintance, or a stranger—tells you about a need, be very careful when you say the words, "I'll pray for you." Don't allow those words to come out of your mouth if you have no clue what it really means. I know we don't look at our prayer lists every second of every day, but people who ask for our prayer really need it. I know that when I ask for prayer, I really need it. I feel very blessed and fortunate to have a few friends I know for certain I can count on in this department. When I ask them to pray for me, I can rest knowing they will. I do the same thing for them.

We all need people. We can't be hermits living on top of a mountain away from the faces of strangers and embraces of friends. Human beings are truly God's gift to us. They help us understand the importance and strength of community as well as help us catch a glimpse of the goodness of God. English poet William Blake wrote a short poem that Martin Luther King Jr. used to keep on his desk and which bears repeating:

> I sought my soul
> But my soul I could not see,
> I sought my God,
> But He eluded me,
> I sought my brother—
> And I found all three.

You want to find God? Be loving and pay attention to loving people. Extend grace and appreciate those who freely give it. Show compassion and honor those that do. Then you will be on the path to finding God.

7

When You Just Can't Figure Things Out

> To be conscious that you are ignorant is a great step to knowledge.
>
> Benjamin Disraeli

If not for the abundance of fine lines circling her eyes and mouth, you'd think she was in her twenties. She had Rapunzel-like flowing blonde hair, crystal-clear baby blue eyes, and a body that would make a high school cheerleader twinge with jealousy. It was perhaps a premature judgment on my part, but she looked like a carefree California chick whose main worries orbited around what skirt was the best match for her Jimmy Choo sandals. I sized her up in about three seconds flat and determined she was probably more of a ditz than a woman with a brain. I was right about only one thing: she did hail from California. This woman was the furthest thing from being a dumb blonde. What she was, however, was hurting.

I met her through a mutual friend at a work function many years ago when I lived somewhere in the infamous Bible Belt. This particular town, like most in that religious block of the country, had a church on every street corner, and it seemed that everybody went to one of them on Sundays—from holy rollers to soccer moms and even heathens. Sometimes church felt like a social club instead of a sanctum to connect with God. Church and religion were commonplace things the community advocated and promoted, so it was politically correct to talk about topics related to the two during work. Saying "God" or even "Jesus" wasn't met with rolling eyes or a disgusted facial expression.

One day this woman and I were sitting in the office building's break room, sharing a midafternoon snack of Doritos and talking about ourselves. We were revealing our stories, carefully choosing our words and monitoring exactly how vulnerable we wanted to be, as we were acquaintances and did not share an intimate friendship. At one point, however, this woman broke down. Silence engulfed the room as she delicately wiped a tear that fell from her baby blues. She took deep, dramatic breaths and looked obviously pained. She was drifting down memory lane in a most unpleasant way. She was just about to say something, to offer some meaning behind her grievous temperament, when her eyes darted down toward the ugly brown linoleum floor. She whispered, "Whatever. I don't know. It doesn't matter anyway." Two more tears flowed down her cheek.

I sat there numb for a few minutes, not really sure what to do. I didn't want to make her feel uncomfortable by pressing her for details. As I was trying to think of the best possible thing to do, whether to give her a hug, pat her hand, or tell her everything was going to be fine, she started spilling her soul to me.

She said she took a detour from Christianity because during a time when she needed God the most and at a place where she was most desperate for him to step in, she heard nothing from God. Her prayers got stuck in the middle of air and space, defying gravity. The deity she had surrendered her very being to was nowhere to be found.

She was married for a long time to a preacher. During most of her marriage, her husband engaged in extramarital affairs. He also abused her sexually, physically, and emotionally. She spent hours every day begging God to do something about it, but he never did. She ended up divorcing her husband, but I know you are asking some questions right now: Well, why didn't she leave earlier? Why did she stay in such a destructive relationship? Why was she pleading with God to change her husband or make the situation better when she should have used her brain and hightailed it out of matrimony immediately after the first punch, or the first rape, or the first affair? I don't know and you don't know, and unless we were front row witnesses to the ten-plus-year marriage twenty-four hours a day, we cannot even try to understand what was running through her mind about the whole mess. We simply cannot determine her thought process and what other matters might have been influencing forces.

This woman looked deep into my eyes as she purged herself of her past, saying, "You can't imagine, A. J., those horrible nights and those wretched days. Here I was, face-to-face with such torment, and my prayers weren't working. I felt God wasn't listening. I felt that he just didn't care. What was I supposed to do? Especially as a pastor's wife? Rejoice and be happy? Start shouting about how God is so good? For Pete's sake, I was dying inside! The hurt . . . the tears . . . A. J., I just couldn't take it anymore."

I merely nodded pathetically and kept on listening. There was nothing to say, really. No words of comfort or understanding could even slightly placate her agony and the horrors of the past that were clearly still ingrained in her memory. So I didn't say a word. I just opened my ears and kept quiet while my heart was breaking for her.

She continued, "I had kids to take care of, and I couldn't even take care of myself. Where was God? Tell me, where was he? Where was he when my little girl had to watch her father beat his wife to a pulp? Where was he when I had to answer the phone and hear the voice of my husband's lover? Why didn't he help when all I could do was cry and cry and cry?"

Suddenly it hit me. I believed that she didn't necessarily need to hear specific answers to the question of where God was. What she needed to know, at that time, was that he did care. Theology or psychology or science or anything we use to prove a theory or make a point could not offer her an ounce of comfort or clarity. At that time, she needed God and she needed his love. And he wasn't anywhere to be found.

She had a ton of friends in the church world who tried to figure out why she was going through what she was going through and, more importantly, why God wasn't showing up in the ways she had hoped he would show up. Some said she was probably committing a sin during this time. Some said it was probably the result of some foolish decisions she had made in the past. This woman saw a slew of Christian counselors and spent hours reliving her childhood and her relationship with her own parents. She also worked through her paranoia about whether she did a good enough job as a wife and mother and whether there was anything she might have done to bring this abuse on herself. After combing through the different aspects of her life, she never felt better or was able to move on. All she got in return for her gab sessions were flimsy theories and bills for a hundred or more bucks. "A. J., I didn't need psychological jargon and all those self-help books and workbooks," she told me. "I just needed to know that God still loved me and that he was still there. That's all." Bingo! So simple, yet so tough to experience sometimes.

Who knew the whys of what she was going through? It didn't matter to this woman. She just saw her life for what it looked like—a life absent of the presence of God. As God became practically extinct in her heart, she became pregnant with apathy. If he didn't respond in her time of need, she figured, then either he didn't exist or he was a mean and horrible being. Either way, she wanted no part of him. I could definitely understand where she was coming from.

After she divorced her abusive husband, being disenchanted with religion from her relationship with a hypocritical and nasty "leader" of the faith and from experiencing a silent God, she left her Christian beliefs. She wiped her hands clean of a spirituality she believed was not authentic, was not anything more than wishful thinking, and was not real. It was a sham, she concluded, and she was done dealing with shams of any kind.

Our talk was cut short, and I didn't see her after that for a while. She remained in my thoughts and prayers. My only hope was that she left the table with some semblance of hope, even if it was microscopic. Sure, I believe that God loved her and still loves her, cared for her and still cares for her, but how on earth do you intelligently and in a soulful kind of way convey those things to someone who has experienced pains you cannot relate to or even imagine? How do you convince someone that God never forsakes his children and that regardless of our particular circumstances, we still need to have faith, when you haven't walked in that person's shoes even just around the block? How do you paint a picture of a God who is full of love, grace, and purpose to someone whose life experiences reflect the complete opposite?

I don't know. Sometimes I think it's just best to keep your trap shut and instead keep these people in your thoughts, your prayers, and your heart. I believe that God has ways of working things out in the lives of folks sometimes without needing our interference, our meddling, and our suggestions, no matter how sincere our intentions may be.

And when you are in a seemingly hopeless situation or have more questions than answers, sometimes it's better to rest in blind trust or blind faith, even though it may seem foolish, than to expend all of your energy, time, and emotions trying to figure stuff out.

Sometimes Answers Are Not What the Doctor Ordered

It seems that everyone has got an answer for everything. I've noticed this to be especially true as it concerns the Christian world. Many know-it-all clubs speckle the religion circle. For example, I have unfortunately had many experiences in different churches where pastors have acted more like spiritual dictators than shepherds. They had bullet point lists as to what their members should or should not do, how they should dress, what kind of entertainment they should listen to, and how many times a week they needed to evangelize. And of course they had a pat answer for every question that came their way. They had formulas. They had all the variables to every equation. They didn't miss a beat in offering their persuasive suggestions for your problems. And you know what? They couldn't have been more wrong.

I'm not saying that we are not supposed to look for answers or think about problems or search out the deep things of spirituality. Not at all. I admire thinkers. I highly respect people who dissect questions instead of quickly diving into a response. I prefer, as a matter of fact, to hang out with people who actually think before they speak. What I'm talking about is what can happen when we aim so hard to figure things out—especially things that are unknown or incomprehensible or incalculable. We can miss something of what God, the universe, or life is trying to teach us. Instead of focusing on mystery, we focus on facts. Instead of being open, we demand surety. Instead of admitting we don't know it all, we pretend to be satisfied with cookie-cutter answers we heard or read about at some point.

This reminds me of the story of Jesus at the well with a Samaritan woman. A woman who wrestled with spiritual issues was unknowingly approached by the Answer. She wasn't a religious guru. She wasn't a Bible school student. She wasn't a person who listened to sermons twenty-four hours a day. She was a regular Jane Doe who was searching for the truth and was being tugged in every direction by folks who were all equally confident that they had the right answers.

Jesus met people exactly where they were—questioning, believing, doubting, or trusting. He didn't have an MBA from an Ivy League university. He didn't respond to people's inquiries using science or proven theories. His typical solution to people's problems, concerns, and queries was to tell them to have faith and trust in God. He always gave people exactly what they were longing for, not anything extra and, quite frankly, not anything too complicated.

I think about the woman I talked about at the beginning of this chapter who was going through her terrible ordeal. All she needed was to know that God still loved her and had her nestled in his arms. Isn't that what most of us really need?

With all the questions that consume our minds and our hearts when God seems absent, we just want to know he still cares. That he hasn't forgotten about us. That he's not mad at us. That he is there and will always be there.

Back to the story of the woman at the well.

> He [Jesus] came to the Samaritan village of Sychar, near the field that Jacob gave to his son Joseph. Jacob's well was there; and Jesus, tired from the long walk, sat wearily beside the well about noontime. Soon a Samaritan woman came to draw water, and Jesus said to her, "Please give me a drink." He was alone at the time because his disciples had gone into the village to buy some food. The woman was surprised, for Jews refuse to have anything to do with Samaritans. She said to Jesus, "You are a Jew, and I am a Samaritan woman. Why are you asking me for a drink?"
>
> John 4:5–9

Jesus was exhausted, hungry, and thirsty from a journey. He came to a well, found this Samaritan woman drawing water, and asked her for some. Jesus's request held an inherent danger. The Jewish people looked down upon any type of interaction between Samaritans and Jews. It was a social and religious taboo. The Jews considered Samaritans to be half-breeds who had a skewed theology. They were considered real, real low on the totem pole of society and religion.

Now add to this already forbidden mixture the fact that this was a conversation shared between a teacher and a woman. Rabbis back in the day were not allowed to speak with women in public. During that time period, women weren't considered much of anything except baby-making machines. As a matter of fact, the religious leaders of the day had many prejudices that were formed in the name of the law. For example, in their morning prayers, these priestly men would thank God for not making them a slave, a Gentile, or a woman. So basically, Jesus was breaking all the "rules," all the "right" things that he was supposed to do according to the spiritual head honchos at the time.

It's interesting to note that Jesus's disciples went off somewhere to get some grub for their rumbling bellies. I'm sure that had they stayed, Peter and John would have deemed Jesus's actions spiritual suicide. I'm sure they would have highly recommended he ignore the Samaritan woman or maybe even suggested he go with them as far away from her as possible. I'm sure they would have questioned why he would waste his time with someone who was considered a waste of a life for many reasons. After all, besides her gender and her faith background, she was a woman who had hopped from bed to bed without reservation. She was, in the eyes of her community, a hopeless floozy. Yet this woman was hoping to find some answers. She was seeking something in her soul. She was longing for a spiritual awakening, but not in the form of what other people were telling her.

After the woman incredulously eyed Jesus for his strange request for water and basically asked him if he was crazy, Jesus replied:

> "If you only knew the gift God has for you and who you are speaking to, you would ask me, and I would give you living water."
>
> "But sir, you don't have a rope or a bucket," she said, "and this well is very deep. Where would you get this living water? And besides, do you think you're greater than our ancestor Jacob, who gave us this well? How can you offer better water than he and his sons and his animals enjoyed?"
>
> Jesus replied, "Anyone who drinks this water will soon become thirsty again. But those who drink the water I give

will never be thirsty again. It becomes a fresh, bubbling spring within them, giving them eternal life."

"Please sir," the woman said, "give me this water! Then I'll never be thirsty again, and I won't have to come here to get water."

"Go and get your husband," Jesus told her.

"I don't have a husband," the woman replied.

Jesus said, "You're right! You don't have a husband—for you have had five husbands, and you aren't even married to the man you're living with now. You certainly spoke the truth!"

"Sir," the woman said, "you must be a prophet. So tell me, why is it that you Jews insist that Jerusalem is the only place of worship, while we Samaritans claim it is here at Mount Gerizim, where our ancestors worshiped?"

Jesus replied, "Believe me, dear woman, the time is coming when it will no longer matter whether you worship the Father on this mountain or in Jerusalem. You Samaritans know very little about the one you worship, while we Jews know all about him, for salvation comes through the Jews. But the time is coming—indeed it's here now—when true worshipers will worship the Father in spirit and in truth. The Father is looking for those who will worship him that way. For God is Spirit, so those who worship him must worship in spirit and in truth."

John 4:10–24

They conversed back and forth, Jesus talking in riddles most of the time and fully aware of her unkosher lifestyle. For whatever reason, he rapidly drew her attention right from the start. This woman was no angel, that's for sure. But she also wasn't mindless about her internal life. She had enough spiritual wherewithal to ask Jesus, whom she figured from the start was different, why her law-giving contemporaries demanded that worship take place in a particular venue. And why did this person say one thing and that person say another, and who was right? And did it even matter?

I find her curiosity extremely fascinating. Through her questions it's obvious that she is looking for God. She is seeking out spiritual truths. She wasn't the type of person, as per the religious code, to be privy to those things, but Jesus knew that was mere foolishness. He saw straight into her heart. Straight through to her pure intentions. Straight through to her sincerity. Straight through to her longing.

This woman had very apparently either listened in on or participated in many conversations concerning religion. In Jesus's reply, he told her the most important thing was to worship in spirit and in truth. This story speaks of many lessons. For me, it reiterates the point that we should not focus entirely on rhyme and reason, or deciphering the rules, or following black-and-white religion, or supposing that if we do everything we are taught we should do, we should get a particular response from God. For me this is a lesson to focus on our hearts, on matters of the soul, on love, and not necessarily on giving what we imagine to be the right answer to people's needs.

Life is hard and full of deep valleys that we walk, run, or even limp through to the best of our ability. Sometimes we simply don't know why we're there. Sometimes we don't know why stinky things happen. Sometimes we don't know why God doesn't show up, why our prayers don't get answered, or why he doesn't fix our problem. Sometimes a surrender is necessary for us to continue in faith. Not by having a Pollyanna mentality and being naïve and cluelessly optimistic but by admitting that we don't understand everything and by simply trusting God that somehow, in some way, and at some time, everything that has happened or is happening in our lives is going to come together for a good purpose. This is not an easy ideology to live out, that's for sure. Having a commitment to spirituality is an invitation to experiencing and accepting the inevitability of the unknown. We need to come to terms with the fact that we're not a bunch of know-it-alls and we cannot figure everything out.

Admit It—You Just Don't Know Everything

You've probably realized by now that spirituality is a very important component of my life. It doesn't mean I'm squeaky clean. It doesn't mean I understand every facet of faith. It definitely doesn't mean I have all the answers. I believe that faith is important, and I try to abide by my convictions. I do realize that spirituality is a very big enigma in many ways. The God we serve is absent in body and cannot be heard with our ears or seen with our eyes. I suppose this is why a lot of people refuse to have anything to do with faith—because in light of the existence of the "silent Savior," faith seems pretty much an impossible thing to live out.

A lot of people call Christianity a crutch. I've heard it said that people of faith just believe in God so that when tragedy comes they can be secured by a false sense of hope that, in the words of an overused and nauseating Christian cliche, "God meant your situation to work out that way. It was for the best." I don't think that's necessarily true. I believe. I have faith. And I know that rotten things happen. I don't think the answer to those rotten things is to naively say God did it for some specific reason that I just don't get and so I should get over it as quickly as possible. I cannot honestly say that God intended, for the ultimate perfect purpose, for the Rwandan genocide to have happened, or for slavery to have existed, or for my friend to never be able to bear children, or even for my father to have died at such a young age.

What I do believe is that somewhere down the line of rotten things, good can come out of them. I believe that God can weave purpose and joy even in the darkest, most hopeless, and messiest of places.

I get into plenty of conversations with different types of people about the topic of religion. Usually I get asked a lot of questions. It's not that I know a lot about this subject. I'm not a theologian, a professor, or a scholar. I just feel very passionate about spiritual matters and am always open to talking about them. I'm up for having dialogue about the questions and concerns people have. I'm up for talking about these things in a real and honest way. I'm up for hearing what other people have to say. And I'm really up for just giving hope a chance because I believe hope is important to our well-being.

I have no problem at all with answering questions with an "I don't know." Because let's get real: I don't know everything and neither do you. If you are a spiritual person, you believe in forces outside of yourself and even outside of this world. You believe things exist that you may not be able to figure out. Spirituality has to do with matters of the soul, not matters of the physical body. Yeah, I know physicians may have the answers as to why you got cancer, or how long it will take for your broken leg to heal, or what cocktails you need to be on to keep your HIV at bay, but matters of the soul are not so concrete. Matters of the soul, spirituality at its core, are imbued with mystery and sometimes even with ambiguity. Who can know the soul? Who can truly know what other people are thinking or feeling? Who can know the condition of someone else's heart? Who can understand the ways and thoughts of an invisible God?

If we are spiritual people, how can we know everything? It's simple. We can't. I don't care how many degrees you have from seminary, or how long you have been a pastor, or how many weekly Bible studies you've attended, or how many books you've read. When people ask you why 9/11 happened, or why your daughter died from leukemia at six years old, or why an innocent man went to prison for sixty years for something he would never even dream up doing, throwing the response that it's in God's hands and was his perfect plan or saying something that doesn't revolve around the answer "You know what? I don't know. There are some things that even I don't understand," is baloney.

Finding faith and living out spirituality is a matter of depth. It's a matter of seeking. It's asking the hard questions and not being afraid of what you are asking. It's resting in the fact that there is a big world out there, in both a physical and spiritual sense, and our finite minds cannot comprehend it all. It's still believing even through the "I'm not sure" answer.

An old pastor of the church I used to attend years ago was married for about fifty-some years when his wife got deathly ill. This elderly couple were proud parents and grandparents and spiritual leaders in the community, and both had a lot of heart and compassion that they always poured into the people they came across in their own lives. While health problems were inevitable, as these two lovebirds were well into their seventies, the wife's sickness became almost unbearable. They had no idea it would be so hard. They had no idea it would be so painful.

This pastor told us of how one night as they lay in each other's arms, they softly spoke about the burden of failing health they were carrying and the toll it was taking on both of them. He had fallen into a deep sleep yet was awakened by his wife's moans of pain. He was used to hearing her whimper and groan throughout the night, and no sleep was deep enough to make him able to ignore it.

Letting out an exasperated sigh, she asked him, "Honey, are you asleep?"

"Of course not," he whispered.

She rolled over to face her husband, and tears an ocean wide flowed down her face. In between heaving sobs she questioned, "Why is God not hearing our prayers?" Her husband rubbed his temple and felt the lump in his throat. He gazed into her face, now garnished with the changes the years had brought—the crow's-feet, the wrinkles, the loss of elasticity, the thin skin. The love of his life wore her age well, and the twinkle in her emerald green eyes that captured his attention over fifty years ago still made him weak in the knees. But the wear and tear of the illness was also obvious. Besides her grossly swollen joints, her bloated face had a dull gray pallor and was speckled with red and dry patches of skin. All the crying she had done in the past two weeks was evidenced by her puffy eyes and the pouches of black skin that also showed how little sleep she was getting. All this man could think about was that his wife was, and always would be, his beauty queen. Sadly, she was his dying beauty queen.

"Sweetheart," he began to answer her question after a long and thoughtful silence. "All I know is that God, in his wisdom, is working in us in ways we can't even imagine. I don't have the answers. I don't know everything. But maybe, just maybe it is better that he silently sleeps in the midst of the storm than rises and stills the storm. I don't know, honey. All I know is that we can't give up."

His wife bit her lip, initially only somewhat satisfied by his response, but deep in her soul she knew it to be true. No one could answer her question any better, with more eloquence, or in more detail. The reality was that there was no answer.

As they drifted off to sleep, he stroked her pale face and prayed they would both be somehow comforted through the unknown. It was all he knew to do. Sleep came peacefully this time even though they didn't have answers and they weren't sure what the outcome of their situation would be or why God was silent. But they allowed the Master of the sea to tend to them as he tended to the ferocious storm and fearful shipmates, and they simply held on for dear life.

When you can't figure things out, give mystery a chance to run its course. Just grasp tightly to the arms of hope and faith in the process. I don't know the answers for your situation. I don't know if your life will turn out exactly how you want your life to turn out. I don't know anything except that even in the midst of life disappointments, hope can be present. Only in resting in the mystery of faith can peace find its way into your heart and do its work in its inimitable way.

8

He Knows

I do not theologize about the redemptive significance
of Calvary;
I link a pierced hand to mine.

Walter J. Burghardt[1]

However difficult it is for you and me to imagine Jesus as an
actual man, sacrificing his sovereign and divine privileges to
spend thirty-three years walking around with regular folk
doing regular human things, I believe he did. And in order
to take on that human form, he had to have worn the whole
ensemble—the physical, mental, emotional, and spiritual
attire of a human being. He wasn't just God in Jewish garb
wearing dirty sandals, but he lived out his human capacity
and experienced the same types of things we do in our minds,
bodies, and spirits.

Jesus was fully human and fully divine. Honestly, it's a dichotomy I can't quite understand. It seems absurd. It seems foolish. It seems made up. And that is why during his life, the whispers behind closed doors (or the taunts directly to his face) wouldn't let up. Plenty of people called him a blasphemer as they incredulously listened to him making claims like, "I am the Son of God" and "I am the Messiah." People were offended at his audaciousness to say such things.

I sometimes wonder, if I was born in that era and was around during Jesus's public ministry, would I have embraced his message or would I have referred to him as a freak show? Who knows? I do know, however, that he declared some radical stuff that clearly took a lot of faith to accept. It was a tough thing to do, and even some of his own disciples walked away from the message he was preaching—his call to the spiritual life, the journey of the inner soul—because it was difficult and it was uncomfortable. A lot of soul searching was involved, and many of you know how gut-wrenching that process can be. It takes work. It takes effort. It takes honesty. And it takes great pains.

Still, many others received Jesus with gladness. They sought him for peace, for forgiveness, for physical healing, for spiritual renewal, and they knew, somewhere in the depths of their hearts, that he was the one who could provide them these sorts of things. Jesus was clearly a popular kind of guy. He was constantly flocked by crowds of people and was always getting an invitation to go to someone's house for breakfast, lunch, dinner, or a cup of joe. Were the invites out of curiosity or out of a genuine spiritual thirst? What difference does it make? It was apparent that a lot of people liked Jesus. As a matter of fact, one of the reasons for the many plots in the religious and political world to murder him was because he was gaining such a tremendous level of popularity. It was making the higher-ups nervous.

Jesus didn't conform to the religious standards of the day. He wasn't condemning; he was compassionate. He wasn't judgmental; he was forgiving. He wasn't harsh; he was gentle. He wasn't proud; he was humble. His heart was consumed not by materialism but by spiritual things, the true things that concerned God, and he tried as best he could to convey that message to those who would listen. He spoke a lot in prose and powerful parables that required people to get down and dirty and really think about what he was telling them. Jesus rarely answered questions with a direct answer. He knew true spirituality didn't come from picking the right answer from a multiple choice test. He was the type of teacher who liked to give out essay questions instead. Jesus typically answered questions with a question. He wanted people to work out their religion using both their minds and their hearts.

As I wrote about in the first chapter, Jesus didn't meet the expectations of many Jewish folks who were waiting for a specific kind of Messiah. They were anticipating a military giant who would be quick to use brute force to redeem the nation of Israel. Jesus was revolutionary, there's no doubt about that, but not in an overbearing, harsh, obnoxious sort of way. Any way you look at it, Jesus was (and is) a pretty big deal. He paved an open road for religion and demolished the previous structures of rigidity that had been built to keep people in bondage and, as I see it, very miserable. He came to voice the importance of love, kindness, mercy, and compassion and to denounce hypocrisy, judgment, and self-righteousness. He came to turn the world's view of God and spirituality inside out and upside down. Jesus came to give life, an abundant life, through giving his own life.

Albert Einstein was once interviewed by George Sylvester Viereck, a journalist from the *Saturday Evening Post*. This reporter asked the genius about his religious beliefs. Einstein answered:

As a child I received instruction both in the Bible and in the Talmud. I am a Jew, but I am enthralled by the luminous figure of the Nazarene. . . . No one can read the Gospels without feeling the actual presence of Jesus. His personality pulsates in every word. No myth is filled with such life. Jesus is too colossal for the pen of phrase-mongers, however artful. No man can dispose of Christianity with a bon mot.[2]

C. S. Lewis wrote:

A man who was merely a man and said the sort of things Jesus said would not be a great moral teacher. He would either be a lunatic—on a level with the man who says he is a poached egg—or else he would be the Devil of Hell. You must make your choice. Either this man was, and is, the Son of God; or else a madman or something worse. You can shut Him up for a fool, you can spit at Him and kill him as a demon; or you can fall at His feet and call Him Lord and God. But let us not come with any patronizing nonsense about His being a great human teacher. He has not left that open to us. He did not intend to.[3]

The divine in flesh appeared to the world to open the eyes of the blind and the ears of the deaf. And he came not with guns blazing but with a meekness that seemed contrary to who he really was, the Son of the living God. But most importantly, at least for me, Jesus brought transformation through his own scars, through wounds that purposely reflected eternal shadows. He wasn't just an upstanding guy who spoke words of wisdom. He was a Savior who willfully endured suffering and a lot of the same pains, fears, and emotions that human beings wrestle with and experience. In other words, Jesus spent his earthly life living in our shoes.

What Exactly Does He Know?

How can you serve someone when they haven't been in your shoes to some extent? How can you listen to someone's advice if they haven't experienced what you have experienced to some degree? It's like an Olympic athlete trying to teach you—without having the know-how himself—how to speak French, or play the violin, or remodel your home.

If I'm struggling with an issue and need to talk to someone about it, you had better believe I am going to present my thoughts to someone who knows and understands at least somewhat what I'm going through. If my food addiction starts to poke and prod at my mind and at my soul, I'd rather not discuss the issue with a mentor who doesn't understand the psychological aspects of food issues. I'm not saying that people can't give great advice or offer profound wisdom and a sense of clarity to someone if they have not gone through similar pains. I just think it's easier, and maybe even more appropriate, to share your burdens with a friend, a confidant, even sometimes a stranger who knows what you are going through. It brings an understood empathy that can act as a salve for the wounded heart.

At one point in my life, I found myself drinking too much. I have never been a full-blown alcoholic, but at certain times, abuse was obvious. I am embarrassed to even admit this, but I'd be a liar if I denied that truth. As a poster child for bulimia, I had a handful of lower level compulsions in addition to my problems with food. Alcohol was one of those things. Excessive shopping was another.

The thing with addictions—especially with eating disorders, as I've been taught by professionals—is that once you get them under control and jet toward and even start crawling or walking on the actual path of recovery, that doesn't mean the addictive tendencies evaporate into thin air. It just means that the symptoms of a bigger issue (in my case those symptoms were abusing my body in every way imaginable so I wouldn't get fat), are slowly dissipating. Symptoms, mind you—just the symptoms.

See, addictions by and large are just by-products of one or more deep-set problems that you cannot handle, manage, address, or even admit. You don't cure an alcoholic by telling them to stop drinking. You start by asking them to tell you about the painful journey that led them to hide bottles of Grey Goose in the linen closet and guzzle them after the kids go to bed. You ask them to tell you about the hurt, the fear, the doubt, and the grief that made them crave the hour when they would be able to drink to oblivion and black out. You ask them to tell you about the incident that made them perpetually afraid and how they got to living a life where the only thing that calmed them down during their waking hours was chugging a couple of shots of liquid courage.

If you are not specifically working on whatever root emotional or mental dilemmas catapulted you toward acting out in some addictive form—whether shopping, drugging, sexing, drinking, or binging—the tendencies are going to show up somewhere else, and all you will have as a consolation prize is another addiction.

Again, I was never an alcoholic, but as I was recovering from bulimia, I couldn't help but notice what a major role drinking played in my life. I was young, I lived in a very social city with a high population of people around my age, and I went out a lot. I drank sometimes to have fun. I drank sometimes to forget. I drank sometimes because I was lonely. I drank sometimes because I was afraid. And sometimes, and this was perhaps the scariest reason of all, I drank because I didn't not want to drink. Was I an alcoholic? I honestly don't think so. Was I on a path that could have led me into a full-blown addiction? I think so.

One day I spoke to a good friend of mine who shared my same faith values, although it was embarrassing at the time to even use the words "faith values" to describe how I was living my life. The truth was that I was idolizing my addictions, because to me it seemed that they had a far greater purpose in my life than God. They could anesthetize the smorgasbord of grueling emotions that constantly pecked at my soul. The only thing I felt God could, or would, do was shake his head in disapproval and question his creation—the messed-up A. J. chick who never learned her lesson. But still, I loved God. I loved Jesus. I was holding on to a portion of faith even during those ugly times. I believe that was what eventually made me crawl out of that pit: a smidgen of faith in a season of dismal and life-threatening realities.

As I was talking to this woman, the subject of drinking came up in our conversation. She confided in me that she really loved having a glass or two of wine after work to unwind and quell her frantic state of being from her normally stressful day. We exchanged honest thoughts about how good a buzz felt, how calming and even pleasurable it was to rest in that feel-good, not-thinking-about-anything-else sentiment.

Then she admitted she drank more than a glass or two of wine a day. I paused for a second and admitted that my feel-good feelings only lasted a few minutes before I was knocking back something else that tasted like gasoline and ultimately diluted my judgment and threw my sharp gut instincts and dignity out the window. And then we started talking about why we were doing this, and how it was making us feel, and how God fit in the picture, if he did at all. The bottom line? Neither of us was doing the right thing. We were, for different reasons, using alcohol as a crutch, and we both agreed it had to stop. Finally we decided to make a pact to not drink for thirty days, which we both stuck to. In hindsight, this pact helped us monitor our intentions every time we wanted to drink.

It was a great conversation, because we were both in a similar place and neither of us liked that place. We wanted out. We knew it was some sort of a false sense of security. We knew we were embarking on a trail that could lead to irreversible destruction, not only for ourselves but also for the loved ones around us. I couldn't have spoken about this to a friend who didn't understand the journey of addiction, or the need to have a drink to gain confidence or relax, or the strong pull of negative tendencies that some of us are more privy to than others. I needed to spill my guts to someone who would understand. Someone who would empathize. Someone who also wouldn't tell me my behavior was okay and that it wasn't or couldn't ever turn into a significant problem. I needed the truth unveiled before my eyes through a person who could relate.

That's how I think of Jesus. No, Jesus wasn't an addict. But he did encounter people, day in and day out, who struggled with the frailties and foibles of being human. And he also experienced the same type of core emotions that can be devastating to a person's psyche and well-being and that can drag them away from ever living a spiritual life.

An addict screams at the top of his lungs, "I'm afraid. I can't do this on my own. I don't know how to do it even if I could. Help me, I'm scared." And while his shaky hands clasp a highball glass full of whiskey and the ice cubes clang from side to side in a melodic ring, he doesn't quite hear the faint whisper of the Savior. He doesn't see Jesus sitting by his side, nodding his head in empathy, and resting a gentle and comforting hand on the addict's back. Jesus, barely above a whisper, voices, "I know. I've been in that kind of place before. I remember when my own soul was troubled. I remember when I was on my knees in prayer in the garden of Gethsemane. I was crying so hard I couldn't get any words out. I was afraid. My spirit was wrought with agony. There was a part of me that didn't want to do what I knew I was supposed to do. It was the fear talking. The same fear that is telling you to drink that glass and pour yourself another one, and another one, and another one."

A teenage cutter cries herself to sleep and mutters under her breath as hot tears form a deep puddle on the edge of her pillow. "I'm lonely," she gasps. "Can't anyone understand how I'm feeling? Nobody cares about me. Nobody wants to hear what I have to say. Sure, I have friends, but I'm always alone." And as thick drops of blood cascade down from the reopened wound on her arm that she started furiously scratching minutes ago with a jagged, broken piece of mirror, her view of her Savior is blocked by the bleeding.

She doesn't hear Jesus let out a sigh of heartbreak, a sigh of compassion, a sigh of personal insight. She doesn't see him cover her gaping wound with his scarred hand. She doesn't see him kiss her forehead and say, "I know. I've been there. It stinks to want so desperately to share something with someone and for them not to understand or even want to hear or be around you. All I wanted to do was tell people there was a better way of living life—a life of abundance, a life of peace, a life of restoration, a life of healing, a life of joy, a life of contentment. Not many wanted to hear me out. Some thought I was a nut job. Some even called me a devil. And all I wanted to do was love them the way they were meant to be loved. I also know how it hurts when people leave you at the time you need them most. It's a terrible feeling to experience that kind of loneliness. The only friends I could count on, right before I was dragged away to death, all took off in different directions and left me alone. I'll be honest. It pained me right to my gut."

The cancer patient lies down in an uncomfortable position while receiving radiation treatment for what feels like the millionth time. While he feels no pain from the beam session, his body in general feels like it has been gutted with a fillet knife. He is constantly tired. He is constantly nauseous. Every part of his bones, muscles, and skin aches at even the tenderest of touches. He is mad at God for not performing a miracle and for making him go through this horrible medical treatment. He is aggravated that he gets no semblance of relief from his physical brokenness even with the constant IV drip of morphine. As he lies on his back and the radiation machine works hard to make sure it shoots out the treatment into every nook and cranny of the malignant tumor, he thinks to himself, "God is dead. I feel nothing except my pain. I just want to die in peace."

The diseased man doesn't see Jesus in the corner of the room reaching his hand out in empathy. He doesn't see Jesus beckoning him to just rest in him instead of fight him. He doesn't hear Jesus whisper from beside him, "I'm sorry for your pain. I know what it's like to be beaten, bruised, and battered. I know what it's like to have your body play a pawn to physical agony and torture. I can help you if you let me. I have already shared in your suffering. Let me just sit with you and show you what I know you are subconsciously begging for—a quiet and blessed assurance that I have not forgotten about you."

What does all this mean? I am not sharing these three experiences to make our own troubles seem insignificant or to show how great and wonderful Jesus is because he can one-up your situation. I say all of this just to present the case that Jesus can relate to you. When your prayers end up in an empty canyon and the only response you get is the echo of your own voice, find some comfort in the fact that the divine in flesh can understand your frustration, your feelings of abandonment, and your anger at the invisible one. Perhaps your meditating on this thought will not make your predicament go away. It may not immediately assuage whatever pains are shooting through your physical body or spirit. It will, however, make the road you must walk a little easier, a little lighter, and a little more peaceful. And all this happens in a way I cannot even attempt to explain or try to understand.

The Suffering Servant

I often think about Jesus kneeling in the garden of Gethsemane right before he was betrayed by Judas and arrested by the Roman officials. Here we find a Jesus whom we don't often talk about because it makes some people uneasy. Jesus knows what lies ahead. He knows the literal cross he will have to bear. He knows the inevitable sting of betrayal that is fast approaching. He knows the hour is coming when the midday sky will turn black, and even God will turn his head from the grotesque and heart-wrenching scene. He knows the stone tomb he will be placed in and the terrible letdown his followers will have to stomach for three days.

This is the picture of what Isaiah called the "suffering servant." We often picture Jesus as a gentle, carefree, stress-free, holy figure who had an answer for everything and an escape hatch for every sticky situation. While that may be true, we cannot forget his humanness. His internal wrestling. His struggle with what was the plan for humankind. He was fixed in the human experience, not as an angel or a spirit but as a flesh and blood human being, as a man in the real world. He was tormented, he was broken, and he suffered. This is what feeds the strong alliance I have with Jesus—his suffering. Former monk and prolific biographer Donald Spoto wrote a biography about Jesus that I couldn't put down. Spoto penned:

> The loneliness, the isolation, the grief of the human heart: the kindness of God reaches out to this as to nothing else. This is what God thinks of human loss: He fills it. . . . In Jesus, we see how utterly seriously God takes us and our suffering. He is no mere God of plans and systems, but the lover of the human heart. Here philosophical language fails, for you and I are not moved to love the Changeless One, the omniscient Creator, the Absolute, the Unmoved Mover. No, we are warmed by the nearness of Him Who is close, Who always draws near.[4]

Those of us who experience the silence of God and who repeatedly question whether God cares or loves us or whether our suffering means anything to him, have to go back and remember the life of the suffering servant. Isaiah writes:

> He was despised and rejected—a man of sorrows, acquainted with deepest grief. We turned our backs on him and looked the other way. He was despised, and we did not care. . . . He was oppressed and treated harshly, yet he never said a word. He was led like a lamb to the slaughter. . . . Unjustly condemned, he was led away. No one cared that he died without descendants, that his life was cut short in midstream.
>
> Isaiah 53:3, 7–8

Jesus was not Superman. He was the suffering servant. The life that he lived on this earth was not a bed of roses. He didn't alter his experience to make it more comfortable for himself. He had a mission—to offer redemption to the world—and he did it through the human experience for our sake and for our benefit. In our own times of distress, we must remember his times of distress. When we are torn between doing the right thing and doing the wrong thing, we can focus our attention on the conflict Jesus had in the garden before he was led away like a lamb to be slaughtered. When we are tossing and turning at night, grieving over the loss of our child, our spouse, or our sister, we can call to mind the sorrow that flooded Jesus's own soul. Whether this whole thing means anything to you, I don't know. I just know that being aware of the fact that Jesus does understand our internal adversities makes me want to keep believing in him more. He is not an untouchable being who demands perfection in order to follow in his footsteps. What he demands is faith, and particularly faith in the face of doubt and questions and in light of God's silence.

Why Jesus Matters to Me

Remembering the life of Jesus—his mission, how he drew people to himself, how he asked the right questions, how he didn't believe in mechanical religion, how he nudged people toward answering their own queries—benefits me in my own faith journey. This is true especially when I get caught up in wondering if I'm doing this thing right. It was so much easier when my faith was naive . . . when I was sure that if I did this or that or such-and-such that God would bless me beyond measure and answer all of my prayers . . . when I didn't have to think too much about the depth of my own spirituality and instead could just imitate Jane and Joe Christian who taught Sunday school. When you live out spirituality in the real world, with real people, real issues, real relationships, and real problems, guess what happens? Questions are sure to come up. Doubt is sure to rear its head. Religious formulas that may have worked for you at one time are sure to stop working. And you start to realize that this whole faith thing is really between God and you, that sometimes nobody can supply you with answers, and that you really have to seek him for understanding and, most times, just for peace.

As I am writing these words, I'm in a time of my life when God is not overtly showing himself to me. I'm only catching a glimpse of God here and there, now and again. He seems more sporadic than constant, though at my core I know he is the fixed variable. I am not. I try to pray every day and know that spirituality is a part of my life, but I'm not quite in the ethereal place I believe I was in at one point months ago. I feel somewhat of a partial silence from God, and for some reason I feel guilty because of it. What am I doing wrong? Am I even doing something wrong? I constantly question my motives and get petrified at the thought of losing him through some error or lapse of judgment or neglect or anything else, for that matter, on my part.

I have to keep reminding myself that I'm being foolish and paranoid. What's the reality of faith? Sometimes you feel spiritual. Sometimes you don't feel spiritual. Sometimes you can feel the breath of God on your neck. Sometimes you wonder if he is even there. Sometimes your prayers sound beautiful and faith-filled. Sometimes it's hard to get a couple of words out that are not cluttered by "ums." Sometimes you can't wait for quiet time. Sometimes it's the biggest chore. This is normal. This is life. We are not perfect people who are consistent in everything all the time. We try, we do the best we can, and the rest we leave at God's feet.

I think about Jesus and the relationships he had with people when he lived on earth. I think especially of the twelve disciples he handpicked. Throughout their three-year journey teaming up with Jesus in his ministry, they were gung ho one minute and bickering among themselves the next. They argued about who would be the first and who would be the last in heaven. They believed in the message of Jesus enough to give up their stuff for his sake, but their hearts still lugged along questions up until the very end of their leader's life. Even after the resurrection, one of Jesus's guys still doubted the reality of his resurrection. Who were these people? They were imperfect. They were human. Though they walked the same journey with Jesus through dusty roads and lush valleys and sticky deserts, they made mistakes along the way. And it took them awhile to "get" what Jesus's mission was.

Jesus had to have understood people's frailties, their questions, their weakness, their doubts, their wonder, and their frustration at the whole religion thing and at life in general. After all, he was the only one who defended the woman caught in adultery (and told her not to do it again). He was patient with Peter, who many times said the dumbest things at the most inopportune times. Jesus chose men with shady pasts and questionable histories to be a part of his entourage. He was more concerned with motive than performance. He advocated worshiping in spirit and in truth, not necessarily blindly following whatever the pastor with the eight theological degrees tells you is the right way.

I'm not saying we are given a free pass to live our lives wreaking whatever havoc we want to wreak on ourselves or others, but I think sometimes we are too hard on ourselves. We are afraid of not living the spiritual life the way we are supposed to; so many times we just stop trying. We are too afraid to ask questions or give honest answers, so we settle for legalism. We become content with a Sunday morning religion and satisfied with a superficial faith when Jesus called us to a faith with a purpose. A faith that thinks. A faith that wrestles with issues. A faith that reaches deep into the darkest parts of who we are.

What does the silence or hiddenness of God have to do with all this? I think many of us fall into the trap of following a set of rules or a specific theology. And when we instead rest in mystery and wonder and experience a life of faith from our core spirits rather than our numb actions, we will run into a God who may look different than what we had previously imagined. Your belief may look different than you had once determined was set in stone. What we need to do is surrender to wonder instead of subjecting ourselves to strict and rigid knowledge and what we believe is know-how.

This is the lesson I have learned from reading about the life of Jesus. He invoked wonder with his questions, which made for a beautiful, mysterious, and challenging faith. And he did this as a human being so that when God seems distant in our lives today, we have something to look back on—the life of Jesus. God's understanding, his love, his mercies, his compassion, and his grace were evidenced in the life of Jesus, a man who was fully divine and fully human. He set limits to the all-powerful one and curtailed his capacity so Jesus could truly endure what life was like as a human being. Why? So he could pooh-pooh our existence and finally see how messed up people really were? To see how grossly people were misusing their lives? To see how desperate and needy we were to dig ourselves out of our ditches of despair?

No, so he could understand. So he could tell us, "I know. I know what you are going through. I know the pains you are flooded with and the hurt that is flowing through your veins. I understand your suffering. I also understand that living the life of faith is a challenge. It's not about doing certain things; it's about depth. It's about questions. It's about searching. Just know, through your journey in this enigmatic place, that I understand. And I will always walk beside you."

9

On the Road to Wonder

The real mystery of life is not a problem to be solved;
it is a reality to be experienced.

J. J. Van der Leeuw

What does your life look like right now? If you were to pen
a mini-biography or film a documentary about your present circumstances, would what it say? What would it show?
Chances are, if you are reading this book, there is probably
an element of discontent somewhere in the midst of the last
breath you took and the one you're taking right now. Maybe
your life isn't what you had planned for many years ago.
Maybe your faith walk isn't speckled with the victory reports
you thought should shroud it. Maybe the God you have imagined or created in your head looks nothing like the God who
at this very moment seems as real as the tooth fairy.

Some of you may be wallowing in a sea of depression. Others of you may be delicately straddling the fence between faith and doubt. Others of you might be dipping your toes into the sands of discontentment. There may be a measure of disenchantment or fear stuck in your belly like the lump in your throat you get when you watch a scene from a really sad movie. These feelings can be annoying. They can be a distraction. They can be a thorn in the side for many of us as we do our best to make the best out of life.

Plenty of folks feel an urgency to wipe these feelings away and disregard the pain they feel from their circumstances. Instead of accepting the now for what it is, they have a tendency to concentrate only on how they can make things better, or what exactly they can numb themselves with that will make them feel better, or how they can superficially exchange their bad feelings for good ones and their negative thoughts for positive thoughts. Certainly doing these things is not necessarily bad. I definitely don't encourage anyone to spend every waking moment casting a spotlight on discouragement or wallowing in negativity until the cows come home. And yet, in my humble opinion, we need to expose a degree of honesty first and foremost before we try to change things or hope for the better or even pretend that our unkosher feelings do not exist.

It seems kinda awful, doesn't it? After all, who wants to feel pain? Who wants to feel disappointed? Who wants to feel discouraged? Who wants to feel frustrated? Who wants to feel lonely, afraid, sad, and insignificant? They're pretty bad emotions to feel. But I believe they are important to acknowledge before we can step out of our plights and move toward a more pleasant place. I know this is an especially difficult challenge to people who trumpet faith and reside in an uncomfortable and trying internal space that forces them to ask some hard questions.

If people who once strongly and devoutly believed in God—in his goodness, in his love, in his existence—begin to experience some life event that makes their faith shaky, blemished, or even start crumbling, what hope is there for those who don't believe in God? And is faith in God that important if these feelings of hopelessness get in the way of belief? Many Christians refuse to acknowledge pain because of the fear of what others may think about their belief. They may get some fingers pointed at them and voices that shout, "See, I told you that whole God thing is a sham. Look at what you're going through. Look at what you are feeling. Look at the cracks in your heart. What good is faith?" Ah, such tough statements to hear.

I, for one, am not afraid to voice my insecurities or my fears. Nor am I embarrassed to say that I don't have an answer for everything. I don't make it a point to be vocal about pain or negative things that peck at my otherwise cheery and positive spirit, but I do make it a point to be honest. This is something that I believe can be a catalyst for the migration from hopelessness into hope.

As I write this, I am asking myself a question that I'm pretty sure I know the answer to. The question is the title of one of the chapters in my last book: "Is God going to take care of me?" Here I am, typing black letters onto a white page; writing about faith, hope, and a loving God; bringing to light some fraction of a journey that I believe is wrought with beauty and wonder—and raising a question that you may have thought I already found an answer to.

"Is God going to take care of me?"

I won't go into what the question means for me in particular right now. It doesn't really matter. The important thing is that I still ask it. I still wonder. I am even still haunted by it on some occasions. But you know what? If I wasn't honest with myself in asking it, there would probably be no way I could ever bring myself to remind myself of the answer. It's disconcerting to ask, especially because of how much I write about the importance of faith and belief (and blind faith and belief at that), but it is what it is.

Many of us are much too afraid to admit to our present circumstances and feelings because they can be embarrassing, or we may seem like we don't have it all together, or it may seem like our faith is not that strong, or it may seem like we are a weak and a feeble-minded people. I don't think so. I think it takes a lot of guts to give truth a chance and let our inner life shine in its candor, however uncomely it may look.

I really pity the people out there who take people's honest feelings and use them as an opportunity to judge others, to interject their own pious commentary in others' situations, or to define people's truth as heresy and question the type of faith those people have or how genuine it really is. We all need to be afforded the grace to be able to voice our spirits, and sadly, many of us aren't. So we don't. Instead, we sugarcoat our anger, for instance, at the silent Savior with a false sense of love. We talk to people about faith in feeble voices instead of humbling ourselves and saying, "Yes, I believe. But I'm going through something right now that makes me feel (fill in the blank). And I don't understand."

Sometimes it is what it is. I feel sad. You feel hurt. I feel lost. You feel afraid. I feel confused. You feel mad. But if we don't take our feelings, which are sometimes fickle yet unfortunately at times very powerful, and put them in an open field to deal with, to manage, to mold, and to work with, they will fester. And our faith may crumble. And our hearts may become embittered. And we may stop talking to God. And we may become more a shell of a human being than a man or woman with life flowing through our veins.

I know in my own life, I can manage my situations best by being honest with myself. It takes more effort than ignoring them, that's for sure. But I always get to a better place when I stand in the middle of my valley of the shadow of death, fear, abandonment, emptiness, apathy, or grief and surrender myself to those shadows by admitting they are clouding my heart. I don't grovel in them or let them consume me to the point that I am too paralyzed to live. I just say, "I know you are there. I don't like it. It makes me feel bad. But someone else is here with me. And I know that just as much."

Am I a bad follower of Christ because sometimes I get torn up by life circumstances? Am I a failure because I can ever so clearly see my insecurities pop up? Is my faith a hoax because I ask the same questions every now and again? Is my love for God invalid because I get so frustrated when he is hidden and silent? I don't think so. Maybe there's a theologian or a pastor or someone with more life experience or a better education than me out there who will tell me that by this point in my life all of those things should have stopped. Still, I know my heart and I know my spirit and I know my faith walk. Sometimes those things are just what they are. And if the God I serve is not willing or is not strong enough to see me writhe sometimes or get nervous or shaky, than I'd rather pay homage to a tomato plant.

The fact is my faith—and for many of you, yours too—is being lived out in the real world, and my comfort is found in the invisible. This road can be challenging, with many bumps that keep us off course and detours that put us where we would rather not be. It is what it is. The key, I believe, is to be honest and keep believing to some degree. A good part of me even thinks that being honest is a form of belief.

If faith is that important to you, what other choice is there? I may not like where I am. I may not like what God is doing.

I may not like the fact that he seems to be taking a sabbatical from my prayers, but the core of my being is alive and kicking. And I, nonetheless, believe in him.

The Importance of Contentment

Being content is a big deal to me. It's not a very sexy topic and even seems quite boring. Many take the word *contentment* to mean just being happy, in this very moment, with exactly who you are, what you have, what you've done, and so on. This is somewhat true. I know a lot of people, however, who misconstrue the meaning of the word to include the idea that we should be so satisfied with our status quo that we don't seek to better ourselves or our situation—that we just sit quietly on our behinds with our legs crossed and our hands folded in our laps with a naive smile plastered on our face. No. That's definitely not how I view being content.

The dictionary says that being content means to be "satisfied with what one is or has; not wanting more or anything else." I agree with the first part but have some trouble with the part that says "not wanting more or anything else." I don't think that definition of content applies to every life circumstance. For instance, I don't believe contentment has anything to do with being dealt a bad hand in life and just staying there because you should be okay with that bad hand. If you grew up in an impoverished community with no real emphasis on education, you don't need to be content in that reality. You don't, and shouldn't, need to live thinking you can't have a better life or a better future or be a productive and contributing member of society. You should be striving toward the bettering part.

When I think about contentment, I think about life situations we go through as well as the general course of life, and

I am reminded of how unsatisfied we can be as a people. We don't have as much as we thought we would have. We are not as pretty as our next-door neighbor. We don't have as good a job as Larry down the hall. We don't own a Mercedes-Benz. We are not as bubbly as Sue Ann from the bagel shop. And the list goes on and on.

It is difficult for many people to stand in the middle of whatever their life looks like and accept it for what it is without experiencing a burning desire for more or better or bigger or more beautiful. We become greedy or desperate or want something else other than how the blueprint of our life is actually playing out. How on earth are we ever supposed to enjoy the moment or fully experience today if we are constantly on the lookout for tomorrow or for the next best thing? I don't think we can.

What does contentment have to do with spirituality? Let's face it. Crummy things happen. Crummy things happen that cause us to wonder where God is or why he isn't doing what we want him to do. When that happens we become discontent in our faith walk instead of accepting the situation for what it is and making the most out of it. So what if God didn't show up when we begged him to—did we learn anything in the process? Can we be made stronger by the experience? Or more wise? Or more compassionate? Or more persevering? Or more appreciative of what we already have? Certainly that is the point of life, isn't it? Learning from things we go through and not wishing they would instantly vanish or transform into the life script we have written for ourselves.

This is what G. K. Chesterton was alluding to in his essay "The Contented Man":

> "Content" ought to mean in English, as it does in French, being pleased; placidly, perhaps, but still positively pleased. Being contented with bread and cheese ought not to mean not

caring what you eat. It ought to mean caring for bread and cheese; handling and enjoying the cubic content of the bread and cheese and adding it to your own. Being content with an attic ought not to mean being unable to move from it and resigned to living in it. It ought to mean appreciating what there is to appreciate in such a position; such as the quaint and elvish slope of the ceiling or the sublime aerial view of the opposite chimney-pots. And in this sense contentment is a real and even an active virtue; it is not only affirmative, but creative. The poet in the attic does not forget the attic in poetic musings; he remembers whatever the attic has of poetry; he realises how high, how starry, how cool, how unadorned and simple—in short, how Attic is the attic.

True contentment is a thing as active as agriculture. It is the power of getting out of any situation all that there is in it. It is arduous and it is rare. The absence of this digestive talent is what makes so cold and incredible the tales of so many people who say they have been "through" things; when it is evident that they have come out on the other side quite unchanged. A man might have gone "through" a plum pudding as a bullet might go through a plum pudding; it depends on the size of the pudding—and the man. But the awful and sacred question is "Has the pudding been through him?" Has he tasted, appreciated, and absorbed the solid pudding, with its three dimensions and its three thousand tastes and smells? Can he offer himself to the eyes of men as one who has cubically conquered and contained a pudding?

In the same way we may ask of those who profess to have passed through trivial or tragic experiences whether they have absorbed the content of them; whether they licked up such living water as there was. It is a pertinent question in connection with many modern problems.[1]

True contentment is not just a naive acceptance of life; it is a deepening and enriching experience of combing through muck, by your own hand and with the help of God, and seeking out treasures, lessons, or nuggets of wisdom from it. It is coming away with something that has truly changed your life for the better. This is doable as it concerns materialistic stuff or even our position in life. But there is another aspect to it that some of you may be thinking about. This is where we get to the hard questions: How do you practice contentment when you've lost a child? How do you do this when you get diagnosed with cancer? How do you do this when your wife just left you? How do you do this after you've filed for bankruptcy?

I don't know. I know it's different for everyone. I know you do it however you must so you do not become embittered by your loss or failure. You do it however you must to be even grateful for what you have learned. You do it however you must for you to be an example for someone else.

———•———

Dave[2] drifted off into a sound sleep and whispered a prayer for the miraculous power of sleeping pills. As his eyes fluttered shut and his anxiety began to lull, Dave began to dream.

The crowds roared uncontrollably and boisterous cheers and jeers saturated the stadium. Loyal fans bore their team jerseys, and some had even painted their faces with their favorite team's colors. Dave resumed his position on the pitcher's mound, oblivious to the deafening noise due to his fierce concentration. The perfection of his fluid body motion combined with his strength resulted in yet another strikeout for the opposing team. The ballplayer who had been struck out conveyed his anger and frustration by violently flinging his bat toward first base, barely missing the first baseman, who only laughed in mock horror.

However loud the crowd was before all this happened suddenly multiplied by a hundred as the thousands of fans jumped off their not-so-comfortable seats, wildly waved their arms in the air, and shouted their praises to the incredible pitcher. Dave smiled. Imagine that—all of this pandemonium just because he could pitch fairly well. His eyes darted around the perimeter of the stadium and caught sight of the poster board signs that screamed, "We Love You Dave," his teammates offering immeasurable smiles and thumbs-up signs, and his delighted wife blowing him a seductive kiss.

He knew he made a ridiculously large amount of money by simply playing a sport, but not a day had passed when he wasn't grateful to God for this gift. So as Dave slipped out of the locker room and into the stadium's parking lot with his beautiful wife clutching his right hand and his son his left, he prayed, "Thank you for my health, my family, and this opportunity."

BLEEP! BLEEP! BLEEP! Dave jolted out of bed, awakened by the annoying bleep of the alarm clock. He reached over to slam the button down. He breathed a sigh of exasperation as his head abruptly hit the pillow. It was now three in the morning, and the sleeping pills had obviously worn off. Why had the alarm rung? He had no idea. Now there was no way he'd get back to sleep again.

Dave stared at the bleak gray walls surrounding his bed and remembered his dream. It wasn't exactly a dream, you see, but a vivid memory of who he used to be—a professional baseball player who enjoyed success. He had it all: the talent, the fame, the family, the money. All of it was his to enjoy, and on many days he seemed to have an endless supply of everything he needed or wanted. Dave never took advantage of his fame to get what he wanted. He was an all-around simple man and was so thankful he had a good life.

One by one, the security blankets in Dave's life started tearing apart. It all happened when he got hit by a drunk driver and became crippled, unable to support himself on his own in every way imaginable. Once commended for his speed and agility, David winced at his present paralysis. He couldn't even feel the muscles that had once defined his position as a top baseball player. He didn't spend his days accompanied by laughter and knee-slapping jokes with his fellow players anymore. Now he lay in bed alone, day after day, hoping his nurses would offer more conversation than their standard "And how are we today, Dave?"

He had been in a nursing home for about ten years when my sister Vivien went to visit him as part of a community outreach program sponsored by the company she was working for at the time. She had gone to see him on a couple of different occasions and learned a little more about him each time. Dave was forty-eight years old. Ironically, his mother, who was quite elderly, was in the same nursing home as he was, only a few floors up. He didn't remember the last time he saw his wife and his kid, and he never got any visitors.

On one visit my sister had brought him some sports posters that were donated by her company. She laid them all out on his bed, and after watching him glow with gratitude, she suggested putting up only a few and "saving the rest for later." He eyed her incredulously for a brief moment and replied, "For later? What later? I want to look at them now, because now is all I have." As my sister started tacking up the glossy photos of star athletes and the team snapshots, Dave clapped his hands in delight, utterly enthralled by her precious gifts. He laughed and reminisced about the good old days and shared some of his private tales with Vivien. He could not stop thanking her for taking the time to visit and bringing him little treasures that lit up his eyes every time he looked at the posters.

I wondered what went on in his mind each time my sister left. Did he bitterly reflect on the four walls that had been and will continue to be his lifetime companions? Did his body expel a motionless sigh when he remembered that all he had could be found in that one room that was not even his own? Was he so used to his situation that he just never thought about anything else (and definitely not the "what if" factor)?

I asked my sister to ask Dave a question one day. I wanted to know if he was angry or bitter or if he ever wondered where God was during his accident or where he is now. I really didn't know what kind of faith he had; I just wanted to hear his thoughts about a life event that most of us will never experience. When my sister relayed his response, my heart broke.

Dave said that there was nothing he could have done about the accident. He had no control over his life in that regard. And it could have been worse. He said that he was not mad at God and never was. It never even occurred to him to take that route. Dave accepted the lot he was given and tried his best to enjoy whatever occasional fun or joy or laughter came his way—like posters, visitors who really cared about him, and people who took an extra five minutes out of their day to do more than just say hello as part of their job duties. "I trust God," Dave told my sister. "I always have. I always will." His eyes sparkled as he talked. What she saw come out of his very being were things many of us lack: simplicity, positivity, gratitude, and contentment.

Contentment. What is it? Being present in the moment instead of wishing for what could be or what you want to be. Appreciating people and things that you may have never paid attention to before. Focusing your thoughts on the positives that are around you. Thanking God even in the midst of painful circumstances. Hard to do? Absolutely. Impossible? No.

Without accepting our feelings and our situations, without the contentment of learning how to live in this life and not somewhere else, without rushing through our seasons and not reaping whatever good we can from them, we can never move on to one of my favorite parts of life and particularly the spiritual journey: wonder.

Why Wonder Needs to Be on Our To-Do List

"You just never know." You can take that statement, just like most things, and put a positive or a negative twist on it. I spent a good portion of my life taking the negative route. I wasted energy doubting myself, comparing my worth to that of a plethora of other people, believing the worst possible things, and even feeling guilty for things that I should have never even imagined feeling guilty about. It's only been in the last few years, as of this writing, that I decided to intentionally make a change. The change was a slow process, and guess what? I'm still not there yet—whatever "there" means.

But let me tell you where I am at. Though aware of my frailties and my stumbles, though conscious of life not going according to my plan, though understanding that the world is full of messes and unanswerable questions and happenings that are devastating, I wonder. I hold the hand of mystery and keep her by my side. I make sure I get excited about things that most people pay no mind to. I revel in possibility. I marvel at the exciting things that can show up, the life-changing people I may meet, the miracles that may pop up at the door to my soul, and the laughter that I may experience that will leave me rolling on the floor in hysterics.

"You just never know"—what exactly? You just never know how quickly your faith will get the boost it needs. You just never know if tomorrow your child will do something that will remind you that parenthood is worth it. You just never know if next week you will be marked for promotion. You just never know if your marriage will turn around for the better in a few months. You just never know if the answer to your prayer is right around the corner. You just never know if sooner rather than later you will experience clarity regarding your questions.

If we don't share and practice this type of mentality—opening our hearts to the wonder of the beauty, opportunity, and grace life can lavish upon us—we purposely miss the chance for it to ever happen. Practicing wonder can mean different things. It can mean spending time with your five-year-old niece and feeding your imagination by running with her in her make-believe world and seeing the type of magic most five-year-olds see. It can mean sitting on the beach and spending an hour just listening to every sound the waves make as they slap up on the moist shoreline. It can mean trading a smile for a frown, because even if the world seems to be crashing in around you, by golly, you are in good health and have found the love of your life. It can mean putting a positive spin on even the ugliest of circumstances. It can mean breathing and paying attention and coating your whispered prayers with belief. It can mean stepping out into mystery and surrendering yourself to good things and days that may come where the stars are perfectly aligned in your favor.

Without wonder, there's no point to living out faith. And taking the journey to experiencing wonder means being honest, being content, and being open. When those three things are in practice in your life, the awesome possibilities that can line your travels are greater than you can even imagine. This is how we let the beauty of faith, hope, and love unravel in our otherwise frantic and questioning belief systems. This is how we let the unknown work in our lives.

10

Glimpses of Glory

Not only is another world possible, she is on her way.
On a quiet day, I can hear her breathing.

Arundhati Roy

I was getting ready to drive with my sister to Wal-Mart one
Sunday afternoon about four years ago. To put it mildly, I was
depressed. For the umpteenth time, a relationship I had with
a man had fallen apart in a horrible way. He was added to
the list of phantoms that had mysteriously accumulated to a
peculiar degree in the last three years, though I was starting to
become uncomfortably accustomed to the consistent pattern.
My bank account was dwindling down to the last penny; I
was planning to spend a month with my mom in New Jersey
at some point and had no idea how I was going to scrounge
up gas money for the ten-hour road trip, which was coming

up rather quickly. This book you are now reading had just been rejected by yet another publishing company—another addition to another mile-long list. I'd had a hideous relapse of bulimia in the past few weeks and was struggling on my third day of abstinence.

Before my sister and I left to go shopping, I plopped myself on her bed in utter mental and emotional exhaustion. I said, "I feel bad. I don't know exactly what it is I'm feeling . . . but it's bad." And I was crying yet again. As I recently flipped through my journal entries and read what I wrote during that period of time, I remembered exactly the feeling I had. I was on the proverbial ledge, and all it would take for me to give up—on life, on God, on faith, on possibility, on the beauty of wonder, on everything—was a simple tap on the shoulder. One light tap and I would go down, a terrible testament to all of my faith-filled self-assurances that I could keep holding on, that things would work out, that I would get the desires of my heart, and that this pain and heartache weren't for nothing.

Being the type of sister she is, Vivien suggested I pinpoint my emotions to a T by writing down a list of "feeling" words I was experiencing. She was determined to get to the root of my ugly state of being. God bless my sister. She had just come back from spending a year traveling through Europe and living in Thailand and was (and still is) keenly aware of the importance of the inner life, of getting down to the nitty-gritty of emotions, and of figuring out how you can leap from a negative state of being to a more positive place. I remember looking at her and thinking it was one of the corniest assignments I was ever given. I had hoped she would say something like, "Yeah, I know. Life stinks. Let's go get some champagne." But I obliged and quieted my inner child who didn't want to do it, and began to write.

Disappointment was number one. What followed were other similarly "inspiring" adjectives including *ticked off, insulted, annoyed, fatigued, distrustful, tense, frustrated, pained,* and my all-time favorite, *rejected.* Granted, this was not a very positive list, but it was honest. In order to do this right, I had to give myself the opportunity to be real with whatever it was I was feeling, even though reading that list made me feel like a woman no one in their right mind would want to spend five minutes with. As I continued writing, other emotions came to the surface. Though I can't say I experienced them in a "feely" sort of way—like how you experience happiness after getting a really good present or having butterflies in your stomach from the first kiss of the love of your life—they were present at my core. They weren't tangible, nor were they overwhelming, but they were impossible to ignore.

Scribbling down the black letters on a white page, I realized I felt *alive, spirited, blessed, reassured, hopeful,* and *unique.*

Was it possible to have these conflicting emotions coexist in my heart? Was it possible to feel disappointed yet hopeful? Fatigued yet spirited? Pained yet blessed? Rejected yet reassured? Apparently it was.

So how is that possible? I believe that at the core of my spirit, faith was tiptoeing around the eggshells of my depression. Faith. My heart was rooted in it. My heart, despite the negative veil I was wearing, refused to accept the unfavorable but kept elbowing me in my gut so I would finally get the picture that faith had enough power to seep through the negative. Was God real? Would he show up in my situation? Would he come through? Would he deliver me from my worst enemy at the time, myself? Though my senses were screaming "No! No! No! No!" my core was buzzing a calm but powerful

"Yes." It would still take a few minutes for me to understand what was happening.

When your faith takes a hit . . . when your hopes crash down like fine china thrown off a high-rise apartment building . . . when your dreams seem centuries out of reach. . . . when a sequence of disappointing situations seem to be the only reality . . . what you are left with is whatever you are and whatever you believe at your core.

What can you find at your core? Who is your source? What is the one and only thing in your soul that gives birth to who you are as an authentic individual? For me, it was the confidence I had knowing I am a child of God, and I have a multitude of promises that walk hand-in-hand with that relationship. God will never leave me. He will never forsake me. He hears my prayers, and he will give me the desires of my heart. He is faithful. He loves me. He takes care of me. I matter to him, and he has not and will never forget me.

On the ride to Wal-Mart, I audibly prayed, as I often do. Well, it was more of an impassioned yell of a specific sentence. I shouted, "Lord, I need you to show up and show out!" Mind you, I'm still not really sure what the whole "show out" part meant, but it was what I screamed out while beating my fist on the steering wheel of my car. At the exact moment after I screamed the word "out," I heard God impart something to me in my spirit. I kid you not. These are rare experiences for me, but I take them for what they are—reminders from the Divine that he is still paying attention to my life. And though it was a gentle rustling of words captured in the depths of my heart, it was as clear as day.

"I *AM* showing up."

And then (again I kid you not) a massive streak of bright lightning whizzed across the sky like a neon glow stick. Excuse the drama for a minute. If you have learned anything about me, I hope it is that my spirituality is not worked out, even minimally, in theatrics. My faith is not replete with bizarre, supernatural incidences. What I am privy to, I believe, are awakenings of my soul from the one who rests in me—instances where my eyes are opened to possibility and my heart is jump-started by wonder. The whole one minute that passed from my banging the interior of my car to the lightning display happened so perfectly that I cannot believe it was mere coincidence.

"I *AM* showing up."

I knew it to be true. God was showing up in my life whether or not I chose to focus solely on my depressing circumstances, closed doors, and letdowns. God was showing up and was in the indescribable process of transforming the ashes of my life into something beautiful. God was showing up and doing things in my life that I couldn't see at that time. I knew good things were on their way. I knew "my time" was coming. Now, what the definition of "my time" was, who knew? Was it a book deal? A husband? A vacation from my depression? Better health? For me, "my time" meant nothing more than living my days with joy, with laughter, with good friends, with dreams, with peace, with hopes, and with my heart's desires coming to fruition.

My sister, being used to my strange monologues of prayer, rolled her eyes and started to say something I assumed would be discouraging. But she didn't. She looked at me with wet eyes and told me that in that moment of my prayer, she heard in her heart, "I have shown up." Why was the roll of her eyes necessary? She just wondered why I had such a hard time accepting the fact that God was, is, and will be showing up; that he was a part of my life before, he was there now, and he would be there in the future; and that things would eventually and somehow work themselves out.

My miracle or my saving grace wasn't necessarily the fact that I believed God answered me. It was that I was able to unfix my gaze from the garbage I was drowning in and be clothed in his promises that my faith wasn't a lost cause—that the muck I had to muddle my way through would lead to a paved road. Maybe not a yellow-bricked one, but one with blossoming gardens of pink, yellow, red, and white roses every couple of hundred miles or so.

I like to call my internal assurance a glimpse of glory. A peek into the divine at work. A taste of the gourmet meal that was awaiting me. In her book *The Hiding Place*, Corrie ten Boom writes of her experience in a concentration camp during the Holocaust. The atrocities she went through and the tales she told are littered with faith. She walked down the ladder of death, and though the stench of the loss of innocent blood permeated her nostrils and stained her skin, she remained convinced that God was there. This was her own glimpse into glory.

It grew harder and harder. Even within these four walls there was too much misery, too much seemingly pointless suffering. Every day something else failed to make sense, something else grew too heavy. "Will You carry this too, Lord Jesus?" But as the rest of the world grew stranger, one thing became increasingly clear. And that was the reason the two of us were here. Why others should suffer we were not shown. As for us, from morning until lights-out, whenever we were not in ranks for roll call, our Bible was the center of an ever-widening circle of help and hope. Like waifs clustered around a blazing fire, we gathered about it, holding out our hearts to its warmth and life.

The blacker the night around us grew, the brighter and truer and more beautiful burned the word of God. "Who shall separate us from the love of Christ? Shall tribulation, or distress, or persecution, or famine, or nakedness, or peril, or sword? . . . Nay, in all these things we are more than conquerors through Him that loved us." . . . Life in Ravensbruck took place on two separate levels, mutually impossible. One, the observable, external life, grew every day more horrible. The other, the life we lived with God, grew daily better, truth upon truth, glory upon glory.[1]

Seeing or hearing God—through whatever means—doesn't necessarily happen on a regular basis, particularly if we are going through somewhat of a dry spell in our spirituality, whether it's the result of life circumstances, mediocrity, or whatever. But I really do believe that if we keep faith and hope and even love for ourselves and God at our core, every now and then we will be able to catch glimpses of glory— snapshots to remind us that our lives matters to him. This usually happens at the times we need them the most.

Sometimes we are comforted by tender feelings we can't account for. It's like waking up from a night buried in tears without the aftershock of heaving sobs. It's when we have no gut-wrenching and twisted feeling in our stomach on a dreaded day we wish would just go away. It's when an almost supernatural force rises up within us and creates inexplicable energy that makes our bodies go about our daily routines and function properly without slogging along. It's when we hear a silent whisper that causes our head to curiously turn and greet the thought that maybe, just maybe, things will be okay. It's when my fingers can gracefully dance around my keyboard and make decent sense of my thoughts in a way that makes my heart leap with gratitude for inspiration.

We are all recipients of glimpses of glory at some point in time. They are not the cure-all for our questions or for our despair, but they do afford us the right amount of strength we need in order to keep trudging through our valleys of doubt and seasons of silence.

Paying Attention

I once watched a video documentary of one of my favorite authors, Frederick Buechner, who happens to be a Presbyterian minister. The creators and directors of this project, Rob Collins and Molly Collins (not related), asked a great question of this popular author, who writes about God and life in an incredibly profound, innovative, and moving way. Molly asked Buechner what advice he would give or what he would recommend to a person who came up to him who was trying to find God. The wise author didn't hesitate even a second to respond with a vehement reply. "Pay attention," he practically shouted with a passion that was impossible to ignore. "Pay attention." He continued his remarks by encouraging people to listen to their lives and to see what is going on around them. "What brings tears to your eyes?" he asked.

I was taken aback. It wasn't the answer I expected him to give, especially as a minister. I imagined Buechner would have begun his suggestions by telling this person to read the Bible, specifically starting with the life of Jesus in the New Testament Gospels. I imagined he would have recommended getting immediately plugged in to a local church and volunteering on the various committees and boards or in other service-oriented groups. I imagined he would have listed out the top ten books that would help fuel this person's fire for finding and knowing God.

Isn't that what a lot of people do? Many folks want to speed along the searching process of a seeker. They want to throw the ones who are carefully dipping their toes in the waters of faith into Christianity 101 Bible courses and place in their laps welcome packets complete with complimentary "My boss is a Jewish carpenter" bumper stickers or cloth WWJD bracelets. These one-track mind people do not necessarily want to gently guide the seeker along the journey. They instead want to make sure the seeker takes a fast-track course and follows what they believe are the spiritual standards that will take them to the right place in faith. It seems like most times they are barking commands like, "Go to church. Read the Bible. Pray. Join a small group." They manage to convince themselves and do their darnedest to convince others that doing these things is what will make God show up or do extraordinary things in their lives. I'm not saying I don't think people should go to church, pray, or read the Bible. But I agree wholeheartedly with Buechner's suggestion to pay attention. I think this applies to all levels of the faith journey and most definitely relates simply to our lives.

Finding God, finding glimpses of his glory, does not always happen by following cookie-cutter religious rules that we were taught in Sunday school. It happens when our spirits are open, when our eyes are open, when our minds are open, and when our hearts are open. It happens when we bow down to the wonder and mystery of allowing God to unveil himself before us any way he sees fit. It happens when we are in a place of genuine searching, whatever it may look like.

To put it frankly, when I first heard Buechner's call to "pay attention," I thought it was too elementary, almost foolish. Pay attention? To what, exactly, and to whom? And then I remembered my life. Recently my attention span has mirrored that of a three-year-old girl. For instance, the last three Sundays I went to church, I enjoyed the music, I enjoyed seeing old friends, and I enjoyed being with other people who were looking for God. But I'll tell you, I have no idea what the sermons were about or what songs were sung. I haven't the slightest clue.

The first Sunday I was preoccupied with the nasty wound on my leg that I got when I fell on a moving treadmill running at a speed of 7.0. I wondered why I decided to wear a dress that particular day to purposely make my disgusting boo-boo visible. The second Sunday I was thinking about where I was going to be two hours after the service. My mind was focused around the particulars of that event—whether it was going to go well, whether I would have a good time, whether I would make a great guest. The most recent Sunday, I honestly don't even remember going. I know for a fact I was there in body, but everything else that made up my being was somewhere else. Parts of me were in my laptop wondering how I was going to finish a project. Parts of me were at the gym because I hadn't gone in a few days. Parts of me were with my mom because we got into a fight the night before. Parts of me were with my handbag, thinking about whether or not I had any gum to get rid of my coffee breath.

I stopped paying attention.

This is unfortunate to admit, but I've had conversations with people when I was so consumed with certain stresses I was experiencing that I cannot recall half of the conversation. I've sat in parks trying to write books and not once paid attention to the beautiful lake, to the chirping birds, or to the squawking geese that waddled by. I've spent time with my niece and nephew and forgotten to look into their eyes to see how special they really are and how much they are filled with wonder, imagination, and pure, unadulterated love. I've had times when I focused more on increasing my running pace than on my inner life. I stopped paying attention.

Pay attention.

This is something we all need to put into practice, especially as we develop our spiritual lives. We can't find God if we don't look for him. And looking for him means lending our ears and our minds to our lives and everything and everybody that finds their way into them. We need to stop living life at a hundred miles a minute and press the pause button for a while. We need to stop fussing about whether we are doing everything right. We need to pay attention.

It doesn't take a rocket scientist to figure out that most of us are undeniably very busy people. We have jobs, for example. And spouses. And children. We attend university. We are involved in training for a triathlon. We are committed to making ninety meetings in ninety days. We are in the process of buying a house. We are trying to move up the corporate ladder. We are working on building a business. Who has the time, amidst the million responsibilities we have to tend to, to pay attention to whimsical apparitions or spiritual revelations from God that just might pop up in our otherwise mundane lives? Who has the time to catch glimpses of glory with all that we have going on?

We are certainly a people who are much too preoccupied to do that. So we demand God's presence during the few minutes of devotion time we set aside each morning or night, if we're lucky. And thank God for Sunday church services. Six consecutive days of self-fixation begin or end (however you look at it) with a one- to two-hour worship time where we are given the opportunity to sing, dance, raise or clap our hands, run to the altar, and recognize God in spite of ourselves. The minister whispers through his lapel microphone, "God is here. He is speaking to you." And we subconsciously breathe a sigh of relief, saying, "Thank goodness, Pastor. I was hoping you would say that. Now is the perfect time for him to pipe up, because I'm too busy to pay attention to him or anything that could lead me to him the rest of the week." You know, maybe that's one of the reasons we go to church on Sunday: because the odds are in our favor that he'll show up, and we cannot commit to seeking him any other day.

Pay attention. Not just in church. Not just on Sunday. Not just during an inspiring talk.

How many of us have actually learned the art of paying attention? We are all familiar with the cliche "Stop and smell the roses." But paying attention is different than this. It's a continual process. And it starts with—and is probably made up of—the small things. Staring into our children's eyes, we can bring to mind the joys they bring us. Holding the hand of someone we love, we can breathe in the magic of finding true love. Waking up at an ungodly hour and watching shooting stars illuminate the dim sky can remind us how small we really are. Through these happenings we can catch a glimpse of a Creator who intricately designed nature and human beings and who is interwoven into all those things . . . who shows us love through the love we have for one another . . . who shows us care and concern through the fierceness with which we protect and adore our children . . . who shows us mercy even when we are not merciful to ourselves or others.

Paying attention means pushing down, with all the strength we have, the incredulous, perhaps even innate desire to consume our minds with ourselves. It means making a conscious effort to become aware of our inner lives, of other people, and of the world around us. It means telling ourselves to shut up and stop being busy and stop going through the motions sometimes. I can't help but believe that when we start simply paying attention, God shows up in some unique way.

Remembering

Remembering certain things can help when we are in shadowy places of forgetfulness. Sometimes a widow can be comforted in her darkest hour by calling her attention to the deep love she once shared with her husband. Tears may flow and her heart may still ache, but something in that remembering will cause some ounce of consolation to ease the tears and the ache.

In my own experience, I know I have moments when I am so utterly overwhelmed by God and by the power of faith that I will be literally brought to tears and sometimes even to my knees. Typically, these times come when I am alone and my mind starts to wander around the life I live, the people I call my friends, the faith that spurs my energy, and the God I cannot stop believing in.

Many times I have thought about the characters in the Bible who speckle the pages with their vast array of imperfections, messes, and starts and tries. They remind me of my own life. They make me realize that when God happens to be silent, it's not about me, per se, but probably just the way life rolls. This helps to relieve the buildup of pressure that digs deep into my heart and puts me in check so I can calm down and relax. God is there. God is with me. God is in me. And I need to breathe.

I think of the safety net, comfort, and grace Jesus offered the woman caught in adultery. I think of the disciple who cursed the one he vowed he would die for, whom Jesus specifically looks for after the resurrection. I think of the man with the demon-possessed son, who has only enough strength to stammer with an admirable honesty, "Lord, I believe; please help my unbelief" (see Mark 9:24).

I think of the thief on the cross who spent his entire life in and out of jail, breaking rules, and slighting the innocent, who didn't blink an eye when he saw this supposed Messiah, whom everyone was talking about, walking around Nazareth like the big man on campus. I think about how this criminal eventually found himself nailed on a wooden cross next to the guy he barely paid attention to, when something tugged his soul. He called out to Jesus for mercy in a last-minute, death-bed repentance. His sincerity was acknowledged and his request was granted. His was a life of carelessness and stupid mistakes that was only to be redeemed at the eleventh hour.

I think of the twelve disciples to whom Jesus offered the chance to be part of his entourage—an obnoxious fisherman who almost always ended up putting his foot in his mouth; a tax collector as popular then as the IRS is today; a man who betrayed Jesus with a kiss as silver coins jingled in his pocket.

I think of all these people and the role God played through each and every one of them, their feelings, and their circumstances, and I am appreciative of the love and grace he wove into these lives. I see my life as a jigsaw puzzle with a handful of the pieces missing. I find some pieces of grace under my chair, pieces of faithfulness in my hall closet, pieces of love in my car trunk, and I remember that though he is the hidden God, I have these keepsakes to call to mind that he is still around. This carries me to the point where I know I am alive. I know I am well. I live, I breathe, and I love life for what it is.

———•———

It's almost midnight. My lamp is faint, my speakers whisper the voice of Whitney Houston singing "I Love the Lord," and my heart beats a steady peace and assurance. I no longer feel the weight of anxiety that pressed against my chest this morning. I cannot find the tears that drowned my eyes this morning. My situation is still the same, and I know that upon hearing the blare of my alarm in a few hours, the day will hold the expected uncertainty. Still, I can afford to smile because in it all, I believe my silent Savior is holding my hand.

> I love the Lord.
> He heard my cry and pitied every groan.
> Long as I live,
> While troubles rise,
> I'll hasten to His throne.[2]

Oh, how I wish I could lay out answers on a table for you to pick and chose. How I wish I could find and understand meaning behind the things in our lives that fall apart. How I long to defend God in the middle of terrible suffering and pain with an eloquent and intelligent explanation. But I can't. I don't even believe it is our responsibility. Who is this silent Savior? Though his tongue may not utter what we want, his scars are sufficient to say he loves us, his children. He cares about us. He wants to be involved in what is going on in our lives. And he is not afraid of our true feelings, our wonder, our doubts, or our questions.

When Jesus showed himself to his disciples after the resurrection, Thomas wasn't there with them. When they told him that the Messiah was alive, he gave no sign of immediate belief, hysteria, or thrill but said, "I won't believe it unless I see the nail wounds in his hands, put my fingers into them, and place my hand into the wound in his side" (John 20:25). Whether Thomas was so overwhelmed by Jesus's death to the point of anger, apathy, or plain sorrow, I don't know. And although Jesus did later offer his hands and his side as witnesses to his death, he also said, "You believe because you have seen me. Blessed are those who believe without seeing me" (John 20:29).

While we act as witnesses to things that get messed up and the injustices that spring up every which way, we are also witnesses to the God who walks beside us, even in silence.

Pay attention. Be open. Be honest. And watch God tap you on the shoulder, or breathe life into your soul, or massage your wounds with peace. He will not hide forever. He will not be silent forever. Blessed are you who keep the faith. Blessed are you who don't give up. Blessed are you who keep believing even though it feels God is not there.

Notes

1. The Silent Treatment

1. Elie Wiesel, *Night* (New York: Hill & Wang, 1972), 65.

2. Emil Fackenheim, *The Jewish Return into History: Reflections in the Age of Auschwitz and a New Jerusalem* (New York: Schocken, 1978), 23–24 (emphasis added).

3. Richard L. Rubeinstein, *After Auschwitz: History, Theology, and Contemporary Judaism* (Baltimore: Johns Hopkins University Press, 1966), 20.

4. Paul M. Van Buren, *Discerning the Way: A Theology of the Jewish-Christian Reality* (Lanham, MD: University Press of America, 1995), 119.

2. Begging for a Miracle

1. Frederick Buechner, *Wishful Thinking: A Seeker's ABC* (New York: HarperCollins, 1993), 74.

2. C. S. Lewis, *Surprised by Joy: The Shape of My Early Life* (New York: Harcourt Brace, 1955), 18–19.

3. The Terror of Trust

1. "'Tis So Sweet to Trust in Jesus," lyrics by Louisa M. R. Stead, 1882.

2. Ibid.

4. Faith: Where Is My Money-Back Guarantee?

1. Lonny J. Brown, Ph.D., "The Power of Belief: Surprising Studies on Faith and Health," Lupus Foundation of Minnesota, 2001, http://www.lupusmn.org/the-power-of-belief-surprising-studies-on-faith-and-health-article.php.

2. Ibid.

3. Emily Dickinson in Roger Lundin, *Emily Dickinson and the Art of Belief* (Grand Rapids: Eerdmans, 2004), 3.

6. Seeing the Invisible through the Visible

1. Philip Yancey, "Where was God on 9/11?" *Christianity Today*, October (Web-only) 2001, http://www.christianitytoday.com/ct/2001/october web-only/10-22-21.0.html.

2. Mary Snow and Ashley Fantz, "Woman Who Died on Hospital Floor Called 'Beautiful Person,'" CNN.com, July 3, 2008, http://www.cnn.com/2008/US/07/03/hospital.woman.death/.

8. He Knows

1. Walter J. Burghardt, "Contemplation: A Long Loving Look at the Real," *Church*, Winter 1989, www.theyardleygroup.com/Burghardt_-_Contemplation_a_long_loving.pdf.

2. George Sylvester Viereck, "What Life Means to Einstein," *Saturday Evening Post*, October 26, 1929, 17.

3. C. S. Lewis, *Mere Christianity* (New York: HarperCollins, 1952), 52.

4. Donald Spoto, *The Hidden Jesus: A New Life* (New York: St. Martin's Press, 1998), 126.

9. On the Road to Wonder

1. G. K. Chesterton, in "The Contented Man," *A Miscellany of Men* (West Valley City, UT: Waking Lion, 2006), 157–59.

2. Name has been changed.

10. Glimpses of Glory

1. Corrie ten Boom with Elizabeth and John Sherrill, *The Hiding Place*, 35th anniv. ed. (Grand Rapids: Chosen, 2006), 206.

2. Richard Smallwood, "I Love the Lord," performed by Whitney Houston, *The Preacher's Wife Original Soundtrack Album*, Richwood Music/Century Oak Publishing Group, adm. by CMI (BMI), 1996.

A. J. Gregory is an accomplished freelance writer who has helped author nine books. Thought-provoking and meditative, A. J. is not afraid to seek out and expose the truth of the inner life—the good, bad, and ugly. Through asking the tough questions, her transparency is honest, refreshing, and painfully revealing.